The Healing Path

OVERCOMING THE WOUNDS OF
SLAVERY AND ORPHANHOOD

Robin Pasley

Find this book online for free on many open source book platforms. Why? Because we want everyone to read it.

Find it online in every ebook format for digital readers at www.bookshooter.com—where the independent author can finally go digital!

This book was created via a partnership with www.TheEmpowermentHouse.com—a coaching service for the author who wants to be profitably independent.

Published by Blue Renaissance Publishing
Part of the Blue Renaissance Creative Group
743 Gold Hill Place
Woodland Park, CO 80866

Cover Design: Kyle Steed

Printed in the Unites States of America

ISBN: 978-0-9825434-2-9

Library of Congress Control Number: 2010908295"

Dedicated to my parents who did the hard labor of tilling the ground of my soul (especially through the teen years). Thank you for always pointing me to Jesus and for planting the seeds that grew confidence, passion, and a belief that God would bring me the man of my dreams.

To my best friend, partner, and that very man of my dreams, Ben. You remind me of who I really am and make room for me to continue to blossom into the destiny the Father has for me. Thank you.

And lastly, to Doug and Rita Roberts who've watered, weeded, and fortified the garden of my soul. You called forth my daughterhood. Thank you for your wisdom which laid the foundations for my soul and for this book.

TABLE OF CONTENTS

PREFACE

I know it might be cliché to start any talk with a note from the dictionary, but hopefully since I'm making the confession up front you will cut me some slack. The word *recovery* was in the working title of *The Healing Path* back in the early draft stages of writing. I thought this word really pointed to the central idea of this book. My early attachment to the word drove me to the Google machine and I discovered these entries for *recover* in the Merriam-Webster online dictionary:

1. to get back, regain,
2. to bring back to normal position or condition.

This book is about recovering our souls to their "normal position." I believe our normal position with God is to be immersed in his consuming love and to live in the regular confidence of our position with him as his sons. I use the word sons here not as a gender specific term, but as a term of family endearment, family position, and family favor. We can all be our Father's sons, regardless of gender, because we are dear to his heart, placed in his family as carriers of his DNA, and we are destined to inherit his favor both in this life and the life to come. To walk in the joy and confidence of sonship is normal once we have received our adoption into our heavenly family. This adoption is a miracle gift from Jesus, and the subsequent restoration of our relationship to God the Father is one of being restored to sonship. The question this book asks—and then seeks to answer—is, "If I am my heavenly Father's son, then why don't I act like it all the time?"

This question goes right to the heart of our problem. We know that we don't always act like the favored sons that we are. We know that we don't always act like we are free to really be ourselves. We could have all the knowledge in the world about sonship and adoption and God's love, but if that knowledge doesn't affect the way we live and act, then it doesn't matter much, does it?

This book is different from other books that seek to teach kingdom ways, truth, or values from a more intellectual perspective. It is different because I have come to these kingdom insights not only by God loving and teaching me, but I have also come to it by failure, frustration, and by finding myself acting like an orphan and a slave long after thinking I had conquered those mindsets. This book is full of my own confessions of weakness, flaws, and imperfections. My hope in sharing such intimate stories of deficiency is that it may bring us together as people who really do need to reach out for help. I know I need to reach out for help. And I know I am not alone in that need.

Clearly, the word *recover* is perfect for us to consider because it points to the fact that we have lost our normal position with the Father and we are in desperate need to get back to our place of confidence with him. But this word recover is also filled with hope! We really can recover. I don't just hope we can recover from our lack of confidence in God's love, I know we can. I want to share my confidence with you and I want to inspire you to believe that you can recover to sonship as well.

This book will begin with a series of personal confessions. In these confessions I am going to be honest about my own struggles with walking in my sonship. The second section of the book will hold up key truths that have come out of these struggles for me which, simply put, are ways to find God more beautiful and receive him more fully. These encounters with a more beautiful God lay the groundwork for recovering to our normal position of sonship, which we do in amazingly practical steps in the third and final section of the book. In the last section I will invite you to invest in your own confessions and engage your own healing process through a series of practical questions, challenges, and investigations into your heart in a workbook format. We will go on a "hike" together and see our process of recovery as a journey that we walk together. I invite you write all over this book, dog ear the pages that you need, and let it become a helpful guidebook on your journey to sonship.

PART 1:
CONFESSIONS

I NEED APPROVAL

A CONFESSION

It had been years since I had seen most of the people in the room. They had arrived at the largish home near Dallas, Texas for a house concert that my husband and I would be playing. I was busy greeting most of them, enjoying the mix of friends and family who had come. For most, I learned, this was their first house concert experience. A house concert is a very unique environment for both playing and enjoying music. Usually, anywhere from twenty to forty people pack into a home that can accommodate them, the musicians, and the food, and everyone enjoys a casual evening of together-time that spills into an up-close-and-personal concert experience. For the artist, the event is either inspiring because of the proximity of the audience or terrifying because there is no separation between the artist and the audience at all.

That night there was a low hum of conversation with intermittent cackles of laughter. The clink of glassware and dishes filled the air as everyone buzzed around the table of appetizers like bees in a hive. The small crowd was made up of a mixture of family friends that I see at least annually and high school pals who I probably hadn't seen or talked to since my wedding day almost fifteen years ago.

We were thirty minutes from moving to our instruments and starting the music when I realized that I was miserably nervous. This was our first concert where we would be so close and so thoroughly surrounded by my peers from childhood and high school.

My mind was spinning like a reel to reel tape machine playing a message that I desperately wanted to believe: "You've got this...you aren't 15 anymore...it doesn't matter what they think about you...you know who you are, Robin...you are your heavenly Father's favorite daughter...that's who you are...just believe it!"

The tape was playing, but my heart wasn't hearing it.

I roamed around the room from one conversational cluster to the next catching little glimpses into my old friends' current worlds. Kevin, who I had a crush on when we were pre-high school, had become a successful banker. He looked well and his wife was as beautiful as she was on their wedding day. "Good for him," I thought to myself. Then there was Hannah. She'd been in my wedding. I chose her to be a bridesmaid because I thought we would be life long friends, but this was the first time I had seen her in a decade. So much for planning ahead for friendship. It was great catching up with her and seeing pictures of her children. Then the door bell would ring and I couldn't help but look with anticipation at who would come in next.

The scenes continued to play out like this for much of the first part of the evening. And all the while I struggled with feeling like a high schooler who might not be accepted by the "in" crowd.

As the night went on it became obvious to me that the tape player in my mind was disconnected from my soul. Instead of confidently listening to my friends tell about their past decade of experiences, I found myself finding ways to tell stories of my personal successes—with the occasional name drop for impact. Aughh! What was happening to me? I thought I had moved past this place of desperation in my heart that housed a need to shine brighter than others and by doing so gain their approval. Apparently not.

It had been a long time since I felt such an impulse to prove myself like this. I had even been in other situations with many more people I might want to impress without having these instincts crop up so strongly. Why now? Why in this teeny little house show—in view of the hundreds and hundreds of concerts and pretty big stages I had played in the past—am I overwhelmed by this need to turn up the spotlight on my own accomplishments? Even in the midst of those stories I wanted so badly to close my mouth and just shut up...but something else seemed to be in charge. Why couldn't I just be myself? Maybe I still struggled with feeling O.K. inside my own skin. The internal pain of wanting my tape recorder thoughts to line up with my actions was overwhelming me. I was desperately in need of my friends' approval, and not knowing if I had it was wrecking me.

A DEEPER LOOK

I grew up in a loving home with parents who encouraged me to be myself. Me just being me was a good thing. There was no conformity pressure in our house, and I grew up believing that being different was perfectly good and perfectly acceptable. This was good because I was a very imaginative child, and I lived in an alternate universe much of the time. I had imaginary friends; one was named Candle. Candle was a quiet, small, blonde haired girl who liked to be with me. I also deeply engaged with books and movies. When I read a book I became one of the characters. When I saw a movie, I went into it and emotionally experienced what one or more of the characters experienced, and if time and space allowed I became one of those characters in my subsequent playtime. Today, it is hard to believe that one of my own children is a mirror image of myself at that age. Xander has been wearing outfits and pretending to be characters since before he could even speak and is still obsessed with living into these characters at seven years of age.

Like my son, I lived in my daydreams most of the time, and because this behavior was accepted by my parents I assumed it was completely normal. At that season of my life I didn't need to change anything to be accepted by my family, my parents, or my peers.

But I grew up.

As I got older and moved into the more demanding social environments of middle school and beyond I learned that this behavior was considered a bit more bizarre and a little less than normal. I might have been able to navigate this tension for quite a while, but it all fell apart for me in 6th grade when I became friends with Sandy. Sandy knew what clothes to wear and what kinds of friends to make in order to be popular. "Popular" soon became a working concept in my formerly imagination-filled mind. Sandy was popular and she was sharing the popularity code with me. I noticed that other kids liked Sandy, and she got the kind of attention from them that I didn't get. Down the rabbit-hole of comparison I went: hair, skin, body, clothes, friends, beliefs. My whole world changed in the course of only one school year, and with the advent of this one new relationship, everything had taken a turn into difficult. Life was so much harder to navigate.

I continued to embrace this new system of comparing myself to others and enjoying the new attention I could get inside of the popularity code. The idea that I needed to change myself to become what was more acceptable by others was becoming less of a subconscious idea and more of a social necessity. By the time I was in the 7th grade I had excelled at living up to this new set of ideals in order to secure my self esteem, and, with explosive force, boys entered the picture. Who knew that the concept of rejection could be so completely embodied by another person? Who knew the master of such deeply sought after acceptance (or such feared rejection) would be nothing more than...a boy.

Sandy looked more like a girl than I did. I didn't have her physique. I was a skinny little girl with big curlo-bushy blonde hair and a nose that was on an accelerated growth curve several years ahead of the rest of my body. I noticed that I did not have the curves that other girls were getting and that I didn't seem to attract as many boys, at least not the ones I had a crush on. I felt like I didn't fit in. I needed someone to give me their approval and to tell me I was O.K.

The fact that teenagers struggle to feel accepted and to feel good about themselves isn't an earth shattering revelation. It's common. It's the stuff of sitcoms and dramas on the Disney Channel. But discussing the roots of why we feel so out of place in those years, and even more importantly, why these feelings persist even in our adult lives, is worth a few words. Personally, I have to get to the root of it because, as these confessions illustrate, I know this need for approval still reaches out and wraps its awkward hunger around my heart.

WHAT I AM LEARNING

Adam and Eve are humanity's original father and mother. As the story is told to us in Genesis our mom was pretty but gullible, and she believed whatever the snake whispered to her. She had an awkward weakness and the serpent knew it. We don't know exactly how much time passed before the devil struck up the conversation with Eve, but we know that up until then she felt no shame from being naked with Adam amongst the beauty of their lush surroundings. I imagine her swinging from vine to vine in a Tarzan-meets-Jane manner, completely enjoying the freedom that was life in the garden until that terrible day when she got her first dose of doubt.

The devil said to Eve, "Did God really say, 'You must not eat from any tree in the garden?'"

Eve replied to the serpent, "We may eat fruit from the trees in the garden, but God did say, 'You must not eat fruit from the tree that is in the middle of the garden, and you must not touch it, or you will die.'"

"You will not surely die," the serpent said to the woman. "For God knows that when you eat of it your eyes will be opened, and you will be like God, knowing good and evil" (Genesis 3:1b-5 New International Version).

Enter the enemy of our soul's most powerful play. It begins with, "Did God really say?"

This angle of questioning is so often the way our enemy leads out in his temptations, isn't it? And that question became the beginning of most of our own questions. They plague us our whole life. They are the ones that we can't answer in our generation in order to save the next generation of their misery. Instead they are passed on to haunt one generation after the next. Rich and poor suffer the same in this regard and no one who has ever lived has escaped the vibrating doubts that were brought into humanity that day. The devil has driven a wedge into our relationship with God.

Can you hear the line of thinking the enemy was igniting in Eve's mind? It goes like this:

"Don't you see what God is doing? Your Father has been holding out on you.

"Well, actually he hasn't told you the whole truth.

"See, you didn't die when you took a bite of that fruit, did you?

"Why do you think he would do that anyway? It doesn't make sense."

Now calculate the thought process that those questions trigger in our hearts. The questions themselves lead our hearts to conclusions even if we don't understand all the details of the situation. It is these conclusions that our enemy is banking on. These conclusions begin to drive a separation into relationships.

You see, our enemy doesn't need us to hate God, or reject God, or to intellectually dismiss God. All he really needs is for us to look to—and then trust—someone else to tell us what is really important and needful for our souls. This "someone else" could be a peer, it could be a leader, an influential crowd, or it could just be ourselves.

Why? Because anything that tries to tell us who we are and what is really important in life other than God himself is an inferior, impotent replacement that, if followed, will lead us to destruction.

The beginnings of separation sound something like this in our minds:

"Is he telling me everything?

"Maybe I can get the rest of the story from someone else other than God.

"Since he is not taking care of my needs I'll have to take care of myself."

For some, this line of thinking boils down to a conclusion as concrete as, "He must not really love me," but for me that was not the case.

Remember how, when I was in the 6th grade, I began to look for someone else to answer my questions about worth and acceptance? Did I ever say that my parent's didn't love me? No. They always did; furthermore, they were always supportive of me and were constantly encouraging me and approving me. So how did the question of acceptance find soil to grow in? It was already fertilized with the lies that Eve had received into her heart. So the moment my heart was tempted to look to someone else to answer a question that my parents did not have the answer to I was easily drawn into whatever seemed to hint at an answer to my question. Sandy was simply "new information" about how to be accepted and important in this world. I didn't know that it was foolish. I did not know that by receiving Sandy's popularity grid of approval that I was simultaneously rejecting part of my own loving parent's grid which was of an unconditional kind. When I went down that trail of pursuit with Sandy I lost the sound of my parent's voice along with their loving, truthful approval of who I really was.

No, my parents aren't perfect, but they don't have to be for the comparison here to make quick sense. The devil simply needs us to trust anyone or anything for "new information" about how to find our sense of O.K.-ness in this life in order to drive a separation between us and our confident destiny in God's eyes. The day Adam and Eve fell for this deception was devastating to humanity's soul. The devastation was not just the curse of death and hard labor that was placed on both man and woman. It's destructive power went much further for humankind. Their independence created what began as a separation of doubt that has now created a chasm between man and God—a traumatic crushing of the intimacy they had shared before the diversion. This is the meaning of being lost. We were separated from our true Father, who alone has the answers for our need for importance, acceptance, and approval. Now the separation has reached a crescendo and it rings in the ears of all humanity:

"You have no Father."

That lie has been passed through the blood line from generation to generation, telling us all that we have no Father. And that is precisely what the enemy was convincing Eve: "There is no one for you. You have no one to protect you. God is lying to you." When our original parents received this deception something supernatural happened that I believe changed them to their core. I imagine it like their DNA was altered and the lie that they believed was added like a strand and passed along to every human that has ever lived. This altered strand in our hearts is captured in a word: orphan.

An orphan is separated (in one way or another) from their parents or they simply don't know who they are. The accusation "You have no Father" is straight to the point. This lie has seeded the soil in our hearts. It has created a condition at birth in the hearts of everyone. We call this condition orphanhood. Orphanhood is humanity's state of feeling Fatherless and the helplessness that we suffer from because of that condition.

I am now impressed with a simple fact: I have lived much of my life like an orphan even though I am not one. I acted that way when Sandy gave me new answers for my feelings of lostness when I was a child, and I acted that way again when I was striving for the approval of my peers before that house concert just a few years ago. I needed someone else to approve of me so I could feel good about myself. I was born into a loving natural family in 1971, and I was born into the family of God when I received Jesus' love for me in 1980, yet I have still struggled with the feelings of orphanhood.

I am confessing these feelings because I feel that I am not alone.

I NEED TO BE SOMEBODY

A CONFESSION

We were ten minutes from starting the house concert and I desperately wanted one of those movie moments. You know, the movie moment where the main character, overwhelmed by mental storms, runs into the bathroom to gather herself. After a splash of water on her face and a brief monologue in the mirror she emerges as a new, more confident version of herself. I kept moving around the house, snacking, sipping, and starting small "what's up" conversations with each person, hoping that at some point my soul would settle and submit to my inner commands. I glanced at the clock and noticed I only had a short time to spare before we would need to begin, so I darted into the bathroom to embrace my movie moment. I was looking for anything that would help me get my head together and overcome these thoughts of insignificance. I wanted it badly, but…no…it was not happening.

My mind drifted, as I sifted through my purse for some lip gloss, to the daydreams I had as a child of becoming a rock star. A hair brush had been my microphone and the mirror on my vanity had been my magic portal to an imaginary crowd who cheered and clamored at my performance. Lip-syncing to a variety of music genres most of my childhood and adolescence had only amplified my inner need for a stage. I had always dreamed of being some kind of music performer. Each vision had me singing to a large crowd, but the scenes would often change to include some variation of smoldering dance moves, a rocking guitarist, and my hot husband who was always my manager. I think I giggled allowed at the thought of my husband as my manager. "Hmmph…Manager!" What a silly plan I had for myself.

But the feeling that those rock star thoughts had brought me as a child seemed to creep back into my mind now: "If I become a rock star I will really be somebody." I realized I had been staring at the mirror in a daze for several minutes. I fluffed my hair one last time, checked my teeth and slowly opened the door to find my mom, who immediately asked, "Were you ok in there, honey?"

"Yeah, mom…just a little nervous."

"Don't worry, you'll do great! Ben was just asking for you…I think it's time to start."

I grabbed my bottle of water and made my way to the living room "stage." I noticed a few other friends had made their way in the door since my bathroom getaway. I waved hello to them as I readied myself behind my drum kit.

"Are you ready babe?" Ben asked me.

"Yeah…let's get started," I replied.

We started the concert with a song we'd played a hundred times and the anchoring effect of playing it comforted my soul. It was odd, however, to look around the room and see the faces who had so affected me twenty years previously. Just as I was enjoying the comfort of the familiar something shifted in me and the impulse to wow the crowd began growing in my chest. At that moment heat began creeping up my neck. Thoughts flooded my mind: "They've never seen me do this. The last time I sang in front of this crowd was at a youth group talent show in the 80's." All of a sudden I recognized the hot feeling. It was the desire to impress and it had now shifted my body from tranquil comfort to sheer nervousness. We'd played to thousands of people before…there were only about twenty in front of me now. Why was this becoming so hard? The image of me dazzling them with my performance brought solace to the swirling nervousness in my heart. "If I could just nail this one performance they would know I had made something of myself," I thought. My self-talk in the bathroom had not accomplished what I had hoped for and now this new thought was clamoring for space in my head. I was now spiraling into someone I had known before: a helpless girl who needed to be "somebody" in order to be someone at all.

A DEEPER LOOK

My parents did a wonderful job at convincing me I could do anything. I wasn't a brilliant student. I was mostly average and sometimes below average academically, but I had quite a bit of self confidence when it came to achieving what I wanted and believing I could do it. A friend of mine in college called me the consummate optimist. My dad had told me repeatedly that I could become anything I wanted to be. In our home and in my mind there were no boundaries for my future. He even instilled in me, without the stench of defensive feminism, a confidence that being a woman would never keep me from achieving my dreams. What a wonderful blessing I received from my parents! However, my father couldn't protect me from the brokenness that was still in my soul. I still had an internal need to find a place of recognition in order to meet the nagging pain of orphanhood in my soul. My need to be "somebody" grew from the soil of orphanhood that was alive in me as a child and is still present as an adult.

I navigated my way through high school and college, like most people do, with the internal drive to become something great. This drive, as I have discovered, can come from a genuine place of knowing who we are in our heavenly Father's eyes, or it can come from a desperate need to compensate for what is lacking.

At the start of my fifth year of college at my fourth university (evidence of a longer story that is for another time) I met my husband. Our first date was playing a concert together in October of 1993. I don't have time to share all the details in this book, but I can say that we fell madly in love, had an amazing engagement season, and were married in the fall of 1994. We actually recorded our first album during our engagement and when we finished our honeymoon in Florida, our car was already full of gear in order to begin our full-time concert touring as married couple. For almost six years we toured full-time, playing outreach concerts in bars and clubs to college students, leading worship occasionally, and encouraging students and leaders in their walk with God. We completely loved the work that we did. It was romantic, adventurous, and fulfilling, and we did it for years without interruption.

Abruptly, however (did you see that coming?), in April of 2000 it all changed when we had our first son, Zane. You would have thought we could have seen it coming, and I guess we did plan on some of the changes, but we had no idea of the impact of Zane's arrival. Ben and I had worked together, lived together, and played together 24/7 for our whole marriage. We had very little life away from one another and that was literally the case until I left the hospital after having our baby boy. Upon returning home and pacing into the new rhythm that babies bring, I found myself apart from Ben and the life we'd lived for the very first time. Being a mommy was rewarding in its own right and I loved that time to bloom as a mother, but it wasn't long until I came face to face with an empty space in my soul.

Zane was almost a year old when we moved to Colorado. We didn't have any close relationships in our new town so I made extra efforts to make friends. I joined a group at a local church fellowship called "MOPS" (Mothers of Preschoolers) in order to meet other moms. It was nice to find so many women in similar situations. In my efforts to make friends, I often initiated the conversations with other moms. I didn't realize until later that I would often bring up introductory topics that would allow me to tell them that I was really a musician and had a career outside of parenting. Looking back, I can recognize that I didn't feel important at all, so I wanted to talk about being a touring musician which is where I last felt like "somebody." It makes me both embarrassed and sad to think of those encounters.

In 2002 I had our second son, Xander, and within the year Ben recorded his first solo album. He began touring without me for the first time, and the chasm of space that had grown from being apart for a 6-8 hour work day became a deeper chasm from being apart an additional 7-10 days a month. It was during the silence that occupied that space that I began hearing something creep up in my thoughts: "Ben's living your dreams without you. Your dreams of music are done. Six years were all you got out of it. The Father gave you children and took your dreams. He's holding out on you isn't he?" Sound familiar? I have spoken with other parents who have heard these terrible lies after having children, too, especially mothers. Have you heard them?

For a couple of years I struggled with these feelings of being left behind and of having no important place in the world, all the while having two beautiful children. Somehow, though, they weren't the answer for me. I tried a myriad of business and ministry pursuits to fill the hole, but instead of feeling better I became more frustrated with my current lot in life and more discontent with the Father, who I felt was dangling the carrot of music in front of me only to jerk it away quickly. The questions that had been planted in my heart in the very beginning were growing again: "Was he really good to me or was he holding out? Was I in some sort of God-school so I could learn my lessons? Why was everything I really wanted at arm's length?"

WHAT I AM LEARNING

The definition of orphan has many layers. Stereotypes and fictional characters fill our thoughts when we hear the word. And even though every orphan has their own story to tell, it's important to remember that stereotypes exist for a reason. A basic definition of orphan is a child who has lost their parents. But when we imagine an orphan we often think of a child who is alone, not only needing parents but also a family, an identity, and a place to belong. An orphan needs care, protection and provision. An orphan struggles to know who they really are or to whom they belong. Their identity is, in some ways, lost, and they rely on others to tell them who they are. They deeply desire to belong to someone and are not sure if they have protection or if they will be provided for. In most fictional stories, orphans at one time or another have an overwhelming urge to find their parents, regardless of the cost to themselves or others, in order to make sense of they really are—to answer the question, "Where is my place in this world?"

Orphanhood entered our lives in two ways in the Garden of Eden. Not only was the enemy hoping to bring a physical and spiritual separation from the Father through Eve's sin of disobedience, but he also intended to plant the seeds of doubt about the character and nature of God into the mind of all human kind to come. When we ask, "does God have a place for me?," we unearth this doubt of God's character.

Think about it. We all struggle at one level or another to believe that God is really good to us and that he really approves of us, don't we? We also struggle to really believe we have a Father who loves us unconditionally—that is, regardless of our failures. If we have ever attended a church service we've probably heard that God loves us, and most of us would say we like the idea, but we still have trouble living like he loves us. This struggle can pursue us even after we have decided to follow Jesus and receive his love for us. Even as believers we still act as though we may have to go out and scratch and fight and kick our way to a place of accomplishment in order to be noticed and have any secure place in this world. This is the orphan spirit at work inside of us.

When we have not lived into the truth that we are loved and accepted unconditionally, we will reach out for other kinds of acceptance. This deep cry for a place in the world transforms itself into an external need to be received and embraced by others in order to feel like somebody. This need, when allowed to flourish in us, becomes what we call the "fear of man."

The fear of man is in contrast to the fear of the Lord. When we say "fear" we are not talking about terror, we are talking about respect. We respect the edge of a high building not because the edge of the building is terrifying, but because if we walk past the edge we will be terrified at the consequences. The fear of God is like this. We don't fear him because he is terrifying—in fact, we know him as pure Love—but we do fear him because of the consequences of living past the edge of his pleasure and approval. Now, in Psalm 34:9 it says, "Fear the Lord, you his saints, for those who fear him lack nothing." That is an excellent promise! If we respect his thoughts of approval about us, then we will never lack nor feel that we lack anything!

The opposite can be said of those of us who give to other men the fear and respect we should only give to God. When we let other men set our safe boundaries and tell us not only when we are O.K. and good, but also when we are failing and have become bad, then we have the fear of man. If there was a verse for that, which there is not, it might sound like this: "Fear the judgment of men, all you orphans, for those who fear men will always find themselves wanting for more." I don't want to think and live that way.

Furthermore, we read Proverbs 29:25, "Fear of man will prove to be a snare, but whoever trusts in the Lord is kept safe." Again, we are not talking about being afraid of men; instead, we are defining the need to build our world around the energy that comes from being approved by man. When we do that, we will do whatever it takes to keep that energy going. If we live under the fear of man, then when their approval energy stops we feel alone, empty, and even leveled by the vacuum of need that is left. And then we must constantly maneuver and adjust ourselves again to gain approval so that the emptiness can be filled with the smiles, nods, and applause of those who surround us.

We need a rescue from this fear of man, from this atmosphere of fear that surrounds the orphan heart. I have confessed some of my own fears of man and I've confessed my need to scratch out my own place in this world because I felt "place-less" in order to share a little bit of what I believe most everyone has experienced. Have you ever found yourself struggling to make your own place in this world so you could really be *somebody*?

I NEED TO BE PROTECTED

A CONFESSION

It is one of those magical days in the year when everything slows down and I find the time to tackle one of those smaller projects that evade the hustle and bustle of my normal schedule. This time the project was photo album creation. I wish I could say I'm one of those scrap-booking girls, but I'm not. Actually, I wish I could have paid one of those girls to do the job for me. Most of the time I feel accomplished if the pictures were just compiled in a shoe box and not just thrown willy-nilly to the back of the filing cabinet. That day I decided that after 15 years of public ministry work that it was time to actually document some of our work and put the hundreds of pictures we've taken over the years into some albums. As I dug through a box of pictures, plane ticket stubs and other treasures I came across a photo album that, to my surprise, was already put together. "Ooh," I remembered, "this was my lame attempt at the Scrap-book Memories or whatever it's called." This album utilized colored markers and pinking sheers on circa-1978 magnetic photo pages. "They should stamp these with a label that says, 'Guaranteed to yellow your precious memories in 7-9 years'," I thought.

The photo album was from our first trip to central India back in 1997. As I flipped through the book I could almost smell the open sewers and hear the bells clanging around the necks of the cows in the crowded, impolite marketplaces. I still remember the first cab ride in country. We had just landed in New Delhi and were being driven from the airport to the train station for the last eight-hour leg of our 28-hour journey. The cab had a lingering smell of garam masala and body odor… and there was an elephant walking in the road next to us.

As I reflected on that long three weeks, I realized it was a pivotal experience. It was not just because it was my first intersection with that level of poverty and sickness, or because it was my first encounter with so much life without God, but rather it was pivotal because the Father gave me a very specific challenge while I was there. Close to the photo album in the box was my journal from the trip. It had a brown quilted cover with gold swirls, and a crusty stain that was evidence that this had accompanied me to the restaurant that served the best poori bhaji, or so we were told. As I scanned the first entry, I was taken right back…

November 25, 1997
This is my first major trip overseas. We are going to be in India for three weeks and what an adventure it has already been. We are here to help Dr. Matthew and the Bible school he recently started in the city. We finally arrived at the train station in Bhopal after a very swaying, bumpy ride. We'd been sitting upright for a full day and then some and were all on the verge of falling asleep. A smiling team of Indian believers picked us up from the station. They were very inquisitive and those who spoke English were eager to practice by asking questions. My head bobbed up

and down as we traveled what seemed like another 100 miles, turning and winding our way from the airport to our hotel on very bumpy roads. I'm still a little green in the gut from all the strange travel food (including something white and runny they served us on the train). Dr. M checked us into our rooms and we set our bags down on the floor. I surmised, after looking at the bathroom, that this is going to be a long three weeks, but I thank you, God, for a western toilet. I noticed the spit stains that we were warned about all over the bedroom floor as I was undressing for bed. Note to self: keep shoes on at all times.

November 26, 1997
Last night was long...trying to adjust to the 12-hour time change and fall back asleep with the sounds of dogs barking, horns honking and the poor man across the alley who sounds like he has tuberculosis. He coughed himself into a puke this morning and my puke-aphobia was activated. It was so loud I thought he was on my balcony. Dr. M has a very busy schedule for us: public concerts, teaching at the school and at a conference, recording original worship songs written in Hindi and then we have two more cities to go to after that. Not sure how much I'll get to write.

November 28, 1997
It is about the third night of the trip. I am trying to go to sleep. Ben is snoring next to me. He can fall asleep anywhere. I think the ability to sleep is his surpassing grace. An overwhelming sense of darkness is heavy in the room tonight. It's a presence I have noticed growing more and more tangible the longer we are here. The Hindu religion has literally thousands of gods and their images line the halls of our hotel; one in particular is sitting in the corner of the room we are in. As I lie here I remember the scripture that the prayer team from our fellowship gave us before we left. It was Psalm 91:

> He who dwells in the shelter of the Most High will rest in the shadow of the Almighty. I will say of the Lord, "He is my refuge and my fortress, my God, in whom I trust." Surely he will save you from the fowler's snare and from the deadly pestilence. He will cover you with his feathers, and under his

wings you will find refuge; his faithfulness will be your shield and rampart. You will not fear the terror of night, nor the arrow that flies by day, nor the pestilence that stalks in the darkness, nor the plague that destroys at midday.

Father, I want all of that! I claim these words for myself. I feel the heaviness of sleep coming over my eyes...I think I'm going to be able to doze off now. Thank you Father!

November 30, 1997

Today was our one shopping day in the city. We loaded up the van early and bumped our way through the many British-established round-abouts to the market. Triplicate carbon copy forms and round-abouts are two noticeable impacts that the British have made during the Raj. Oh, and driving on the left side of the road. The rest is questionable.

We walked in and out of stores for hours amid beautiful bright textiles, iron work and cows. Yes, cows. They just walk around with the people...one walked into a jewelry store as we left and pooped on the floor...culture shock for sure. We were almost done with our shopping and had one more street to saunter down before we met up at the restaurant for lunch. This street was busier than the other ones. Ben had just let go of my hand to walk closer to a booth with musical instruments when I felt someone behind me. A man came up on my heels and groped me. He had his hand on my body! Oh my gosh! I screamed an expletive unbecoming of a Christian missionary, and Ben darted right back to me as I started crying. I turned around and couldn't see who it was exactly. Ben held me close and Dr. M ran over to see what had happened. It was a terrible feeling...the violation.

The raw nature of the culture had just taken advantage of me. And now, laying here in bed, I still can't shake the nauseous feeling I've had since that happened. Again I struggle with sleep. I open my Bible again to the same scripture from Psalm 91: "You will not fear the terror of night, nor the arrow that flies by day."

"Father, why did you let that happen to me today? You said that I would not fear the terror of night, and I surely felt the arrow that flew by day!" I'm whisper-shouting because the gifted one is sleeping next to me. I haven't been able to sense the presence of the Holy Spirit at all up to this point. I am so desperate to sense the Father with me.

All of a sudden, I have an impression in my heart: "Do you believe even when you can't feel?" There have been other times in my life that I haven't felt the Lord, but this is the first time I have pressed in this hard with no interaction. I feel utterly alone. Even with my husband sleeping peacefully next to me, I feel so forsaken. I am challenged in a place of my faith that I have never visited—believing with nothing to cling to but the choice in my own heart to have faith in the words I read.

I re-read Psalm 91 aloud so I can hear myself say the words (right now I'm thankful for Ben's sleeping gift!). At home this would have been rote, but right now these are words of life piercing my soul. I speak them over myself as truth.

"He is my refuge, my fortress, my God in whom I trust."

I continue reading the next several chapters with the same fervor. I read all the way through Psalm 100 ending with verse 5, "For the Lord is good and his love endures forever; his faithfulness continues through all generations."

As the words leave my lips I hear a phrase go through my mind.

"Do you believe that?"

With my newfound zeal I respond to it immediately, "YES!"

A moment passes and now I feel what I had been missing; a warmth came over my body, starting at my chest. And as I melt into what I know is the presence of my Father I hear another phrase: "If I take your husband from you…am I good?" My heart stops. He knows me so well. He knows this is one of the fears I have struggled with since we met. I began to weep and quietly wail into my pillow as I imagine the loss. I pull my face off my pillow after what feels like 30 minutes has passed. I blow my nose and sit up as if to meet him face to face.

"You would still be good."

I sigh, trying not to think on those things again, when I hear another phrase: "What if I took your sons…would I still be good?" I am stunned. He knows! He knows that in the prayer meeting just before we left I had received a prophecy that the Father was going to give me and Ben sons. Tears stream down my face as I imagine losing something so precious. I know this is only a fraction of the pain I would feel in that circumstance, since these boys haven't even been born yet. The Father's question took my mind to so many places, but after I consider it I answer.

"Yes…you would still be good."

As I cry silently, I feel the presence of the Father even more near me. My head is throbbing from the crying…I think I'll try to sleep now…

I didn't expect Photo Album Day to be so tearful. I was snotty after reading that. Something happened in my heart that night in India. The Father and I moved into a new place. I gained a new level of faith after I was faced with those terrible questions. It makes me think of so many friends who struggle with the same question:

When we encounter tragic loss, is the Father still good?

A DEEPER LOOK

When I was pregnant with Zane I asked the Father if he wanted to speak to me in any way during my pregnancy (with it being a unique time in my life I thought it was a poignant question). To my surprise he answered very specifically. He impressed on my heart that soon after Zane's birth he would tell me something important. That day came only two weeks later.

It was the morning after our little boy had arrived. Ben had gone to take a walk and get some breakfast. I was laying in the hospital bed holding Zane and I felt the Holy Spirit remind my heart that he had something to tell me. I invited his presence into the room and asked him what he wanted to tell me. It came so clear and so strong it completely overwhelmed me. He said, "Do you feel how much you love your son?"

"Yes," I replied as I looked at Zane's squenchy little face.

"I have a son, too," he said, "and I love him as much and even more." Then he asked, "Do you see how innocent your son appears right now?"

"Yes."

"My Son was truly innocent. No sin ever entered him. Yet I allowed the most wicked of plans be brought against him and I allowed the most evil transgressions be laid on him…as if they were his very own."

I was sick in my stomach as I imagined someone doing anything evil around my baby, much less subjecting his innocence to such wickedness. And then it all came together for me…The Father allowed all of that offense to be laid on his innocent boy. And moreover, his Son chose to receive it all; he received it all for me! And then I heard him, "Yes, Robin. I did it for you." I heard it in harmony, the Father and the Son speaking to my heart that they had suffered together for me. I wept and wept at the thought. His deep love for me…the Father's and the son's. The pain and loss the Father suffered for his Son. The agony and torture that he subjected his own heart to as the sin and utter wickedness of the world was worn by his own Son. And all of that was just for me.

I had heard the message of Christ's sacrifice for us my whole life, but this impacted my heart unlike any other time before. That day I understood that the Father had experienced a tragic loss as well. He had suffered along with Jesus in order to be with me again.

WHAT I AM LEARNING

Remember the seeds of doubt that were planted in the soil of our disobedience? The lies that accompanied our separation from God spoken to us about God's character? They question whether God is really good. They question his heart for us. This attack on our relationship with the Father is a direct byproduct of being spiritual orphans. This attack seems to have teeth that hang on even after we choose to believe in Jesus and receive his resurrection power to forgive us of our sins. Why? Because so many of our life experiences are unfair and painful whether we are Christians or not, and these experiences are used by the enemy as part of his attack on the heart of God for us.

Questioning the goodness of the Father is one of the enemy's greatest weapons of warfare on our hearts. He is scheming and sly. He knows that if he simply speaks the lies he can be argued with, but if he whispers near our difficult life experiences, then our already orphan-

influenced minds will connect the dots and do most of the dirty work
for him. And we have ample opportunities in this life for the devil to
whisper these words of doubt. We are abused in our youth and he
whispers. Our sexuality is defiled when we were still innocent and he
whispers. Our parents divorce and he whispers. We pray for Mom's
healing and she dies anyway, and the enemy whispers. Our spouse has
violated our marriage agreement, and the enemy whispers. If there is not
a louder voice of truth, the whispers combine to form a shout that
shakes our soul and shapes our outlook on the whole of our lives. Those
of us who are still willing to believe and trust him even after these
sufferings often can trust in his goodness for others, but find ourselves
struggling to hope in his goodness for ourselves.

All of these personal violations sometimes seem to pale in light of
the greatest sufferings of humanity. We question if the Father overlooks
human trafficking, slavery, terrorism, intense poverty, disease, natural
disasters, and the wickedness in government leadership that results in
genocide, rape, and child soldier-slaves. When we see with the eyes of
man, it seems there is no loving Father watching over those who suffer
in these ways. In the mind of the orphan we aren't sure if he cares
enough to move. So we make excuses for him or we change our theology
to make him nicer. Or worse, we amend our theology to make him play
well with others by becoming as impotent and uncaring as the rest of the
world's deities. This, by the way, is the spirit of antichrist at work in our
culture, because it is this spirit that dethrones God and makes Christ
like any other god-spirit option in the world.

When we allow our experiences to speak to us about the nature of
God, we've done the enemy's work for him. Our brains have been doing
the devil's math for generations: "If he allowed this, then he must not be
good."

Look, it's simple. If the enemy can get us to agree with him that the
Father isn't that good, then it reduces our ability to receive his love. This
is the enemy's end game: to keep us from receiving the Father's love and
from knowing who we really are, and this is destruction to the dreams of
God.

We must hope for the dreams of God to be restored by asking the
Father what he is also suffering. The accusation of the enemy is that we

suffer alone while God is cushioned in the heavens. That is not what God revealed to me at the birth of my first son. We must let God answer these questions:

"Where were you during the pain and suffering?

"Why didn't you answer our prayer for healing?

"What were you doing while I was being violated?"

He's not afraid of the questions. You might be surprised by the answers. The prophet Isaiah said about Jesus 400 years before he came to earth, "He was despised and rejected by men, a man of sorrows, and familiar with suffering. Like one from whom men hide their faces he was despised, and we esteemed him not" (Isaiah 53:3). Jesus has not just met sorrow, but has become friends with it. He is familiar with it, acquainted with it like a comrade, and did not reject the sorrow that his love for us would bring. The Father and the Son both suffered on our behalf, and they continue to suffer for us as they watch over us. If we could touch the depth of God's suffering for us when we suffer ourselves, maybe we would not assume against his character when he allows us to suffer?

I still need to be protected. Have you felt this need as well? Have you ever struggled to believe that God was good? Good enough to protect you? If he is not good enough, we will certainly look to someone or something else to do it for him.

I NEED TO BE ACCEPTED

A CONFESSION

We were on the last leg of an eleven week tour with our two boys who were 5 and 7 years of age during the summer of 2007. This was our first big tour attempt where they would be along with us for the whole trip. In order to survive the cross country adventure God had blessed us with a 32' long 1986 Fleetwood Bounder RV. That was some serious styling! Knowing it would be our home for two thirds of the summer I decided to redecorate the interior. I updated it from the circa 1975 style to a non-date specific mixture of espresso, brick red and turquoise...1970's style faux fur was integrated. Some very thoughtful friends had donated the RV to us and it became our home away from home for the duration of an amazing trip from Colorado to Texas, through the northern states and across the country, all the way down the eastern seaboard into the great American south. We'd been on the road for 9 weeks already and at this moment we were loading our gear into the home that was to be our concert venue for the evening.

Now, prepping to play a concert has always been one of my least favorite things. If I were to be honest I would say that I prefer more of a Barbara Streisand approach to concert performance. The Babs version is where I am so awesome that I can just show up right before the lights come up, drop my fur backstage, and walk on the stage as someone hands me my microphone. Of course, I don't have Babs' skills nor someone who would hand me my microphone, which is probably why I must suffer the tedious act of set up, sound check, as well as the after concert break-down.

I was behind my drum set plugging in microphones when I heard my name spoken by a vaguely familiar voice. I stood up to see who it was, shocked to see the eyes of an old friend.

"Leilah...whu...what are you doing here?"

I had last seen her during a very wild season of my life—Can anyone say, "Party University?" Leilah's brother had lived in the same house as a guy I dated in college and she hung out there all the time. In an instant, a film roll went through my mind of every single time she had seen me tipsy, intoxicated...and wild. It was more than a couple times. I blushed immediately as the scenes played out in my memories.

"I live here in town and my friend Christina invited me to come," she responded. Christina was the hostess of our house concert.

"Wow, it's been what...15 years?" I asked.

"Yeah, at least."

After 5 more minutes of small talk I found a way to excuse myself back out to the RV and clear my head.

My days at Baylor University had hosted most of my personal challenges to the list of do's and don'ts I had received as a child. I headed to the back of the Bounder to busy myself and try to distract myself from the drunken college flashbacks with other work. As I sat on the bed in the back of the RV folding laundry, I was transported back to Waco, Texas. I'd transferred to Baylor as a sophomore and quickly found a place to fit in because there were so many Baptist kids who'd grown up in a church environment just like mine. I'd never been around so many people who had been raised with the same "code" as me and had figured out a way to party like it was an Olympic sport.

I attended my first party where there was alcohol when I was at Baylor and I expected, much as I had in high school, to find people passed out left and right, slobbery and out of control. Instead I found the same kind of people I had grown up with acting relatively normal and having a good time. I was 21 and decided that since I was the legal age I would certainly permit myself the same pleasures. That night was so much fun and not at all scary like I had thought it would be. One night, after a few more weeks in my new environment and a few more harmless parties, I sat alone in my dorm room, feeling guilty for drinking but conflicted because the fun I was experiencing felt so innocent. I realized I was having more fun at these parties than I did at church youth group meetings, so I challenged the Father: "I know that you said you came to give me abundant life, but I feel like my life with you has been about me pursuing you and doing lots of work to be right. I feel like I'm alive when I'm with my new friends…way more alive than I've felt with you. So if you really came to give me abundant life, then I want you to come and pursue me for a change. I am going to do the things that feel fun to me and if you want me you can come and get me." That may sound sassy, but that is exactly how I felt. I was tired of Christianity, and I was hungry for real life. That night was pivotal for me. Up to then I had not been drunk, but shortly after drawing that line in the sand I gave in to the lifestyle of my friends more and more.

Even while I was letting loose, I could always find a little time for guilt or judgment. One night while I was with my new friends I saw a girl at a bar sitting on a guy's lap. I remember feeling so sorry for her because she seemed so pathetic and needy. From her actions I was sure she was going to sleep with him that night and I wondered if she would feel ashamed the next day or if she had gotten used to feeling pathetic. It was only 9 months later that I was sitting on a guy's lap in a bar, drunk, and feeling needy. I remembered the girl I'd seen and judged earlier.

Thankfully, my upbringing and the prayers of my mother prevented me from having sex with men that I met in bars, but still I hung on this boy in the same sort of pathetic way as that other girl I had judged. I so wanted to fill that emptiness in my heart, too. I guess we weren't really that different.

Seven days later the Father, through a series of incredible events, miraculously arrested my attention and began speaking to me about his undeniable love for me. He began to convince me that he would indeed pursue me and indeed show me that he had an abundant life for me that was even more than what I had been investing in. It was the first time that I remembered sensing his desire to just be near me and not expect something from me. I remember thinking that surely I would have to "pay" for my rebellious actions. I honestly expected to suffer for quite a while before he would give me the desires of my heart. In high school I memorized Psalm 37:4, "Delight yourself in the Lord and he will give you the desires of your heart." I knew I hadn't been "delighting myself in the Lord," so I didn't expect him to give me the desires of my heart until I had done some serious repenting and suffering.

But God destroyed my expectations. He destroyed them when he treated me like a loved daughter and not like the "lucky to be here" orphan that I had been acting like. Within two months I had met my husband, fallen in love, and had begun performing music with him, which was a literal dream come true. Two of the greatest desires of my heart had been completely met in my husband and in a music career, and I hadn't "paid" for anything. How unbelievable it felt to be loved so unconditionally, and to have been able to prove God's unconditional love for myself.

I finished putting the laundry away and stepped into the bathroom (the only truly separated room in the RV) and sat down on the tiny little toilet lid so I could gather my thoughts before returning to the awkward conversations that lay ahead for the night. Would Leilah believe that I am a new person or the same person she knew in college? Would she see me as a tainted person who was hiding the real me just as I had seen myself for so long?

A DEEPER LOOK

I gave my life to Jesus when I was in 4th grade. It was the day that Mount St. Helens erupted. I remember this because my Sunday school teacher told me to remember the date I was saved so I would never forget it. Volcanic eruptions are perfect for that. The church fellowship we attended had many good Bible teachers. Their teachings were Bible focused and always pointed us to Jesus. This was good for me for many reasons, especially because it focused my mind on scripture memory and being able to recite passages from the Bible. It even paid to know the Bible! I earned money for our youth group trips by reciting scriptures to youth leaders and getting a proverbial gold star. I memorized whole passages and was a whiz at the "Sword Drills," where we competed to see who could find scripture passages the fastest.

This is the point where I feel a bit awkward recounting my story because although there were wonderful truths set into my foundation in those years there were faulty stones set in there as well. It is awkward because I don't want to bring judgment to anyone who was trying their best to love me during that time, but I have to talk about what wasn't quite right in order to reveal my own heart to you better. Some of these faulty ideas have created huge tensions and problems in my walk with God. Those leaders, teachers, parents and friends who cared for my soul weren't trying to trip me up, but the doctrine they were (and some still are) teaching contributed to me losing my way with God while I was in college.

In the midst of memorizing scripture I learned that our greatest value as the people of God was to learn what not to do and what to do, and how often to do it. I learned that I would be forgiven for breaking the rules, but there was a measure of shame and distance that other Christians could apply to you for confessing those sins. The bigger the sin, the closer you could get to being cut off from relationship with others. Now, the "don'ts" began at the Ten Commandments, and who is going to argue with those? But those were not enough for us. We needed a much longer list that would cover all the bad stuff like dancing, drinking, smoking, cussing, having sex, thinking about sex, thinking about thinking about sex, and dating boys who did any of the above.

Then there were also the rules that applied to all the "bad" spiritual things like speaking in tongues, praying for healing, prophecy, having visions, hearing God speak, physical demonstrations of the Holy Spirit of any kind that didn't include sitting perfectly still, and any expressions of emotion…at all…in worship.

The list of "do's" was just as exhaustive and dealt with generally good stuff like attending church services, praying, reading the Bible, spending time with God, sharing the truth of Jesus with others. Most of the "do's" didn't come particularly naturally, but with a little effort you could be accomplished at least to the first level of approval in Christian culture. To really excel, however, you had to get good at not only avoiding the "don't" list (or at least at hiding your infractions), but you also had to excel at doing all the good stuff.

The breakdown for me came with trying to measure these things and always trying to know what was the most right action in any situation. Church is where we learned how to constantly upgrade and refine the exact divisions of right and wrong for each other. I remember an argument breaking out at a youth retreat over which was better: having a "quiet time" with Jesus in the morning or at night. I am pretty sure that morning won that round. How often and how much we read the Bible, prayed, attended church services, and witnessed to others was of great importance to our sense of well-being. We were building our own righteousness.

That kind of mentality couldn't help but build a conditional environment that, for me, reinforced a sense of self-judgment and unworthiness in the eyes of God. This kind of judgment was the atmosphere of my life around church people, and it was reinforced at every turn by the teaching and ideas of our culture. This created a cloud of judgment—self-judgment. What the Father thought about me plus what I thought about me plus what I thought others thought about me equalled self-judgment. This kind of atmosphere helped me choose what was good or bad and, in turn, which action would take me closer or farther away from the Lord. Now, our heavenly Father never said my nearness to him was dependent on these things, but somehow I was able to gather this together from my tradition. I am not the only one, am I?

In all of my youth I never heard anyone tell me that I was my Father's favorite daughter. I never heard any kind of love language like that at all. Even if I had heard it I don't know if I would have believed it, since my status as "Dad's favorite" would have had nothing to do with what I did or didn't do. How could that work? What I knew was that if I knew the right doctrine, could espouse the correct theology, and didn't stray from it, then I was "right" with God. That was all I needed. As a result, life with Christ became a hill. He was at the top and I started at the bottom. Nearness to Christ and the Father had to do with work, actions, and behavior that propelled me up the hill. With each good behavior I moved up a level, closer to him. With each bad behavior I moved down a notch. Each mistake left me feeling as though I had lost footing again and the hill ahead had just gotten steeper. Only the strong survive was the basic message we would tell each other with Christian songs and sayings.

There is a particular memory I have of how this played out in me. I had recently been on a youth group retreat and rededicated my life to the Lord. Rededication is what we did regularly to absolve ourselves of seasons of imperfection; it involved a public repentance for being generally bad and choosing to act right again and follow Jesus properly. After the retreat, I had been having consistent quiet times and keeping my thoughts and actions in line with the "do's" as much as I could. One night after youth group we all went to a friend's house and were watching movies, swimming, snacking and just hanging out. A boy that I was attracted to was there and as the night went on he and I found a dark corner of the yard and began kissing. In the moment I was elated… he was so cute…and my need to be accepted had already been pegging the meter during the night, so kissing this boy was very satisfying to my soul. I went home, however, and woke up the next morning with the most terrible feeling. I actually entertained and believed the thought that I had been doing so good, but now I had really slipped up and would have to make up all that I had lost.

No wonder my life in Christ felt like a roller coaster. To me, God was keeping score in his love register and I was never sure if I was in the red or in the black. I was enslaved to a system of performance. This is what it means to be a spiritual slave. I definitely was one. Have you ever struggled with performing to feel O.K. with God? If so, you have been a spiritual slave as well.

WHAT I AM LEARNING

We got a two-for-one deal in the garden of Eden when we flopped the trust-test. Not only did we receive the seeds of fatherlessness, which created an orphan spirit in each of us, but we also gorged on the tree of the knowledge of good and evil, which put judgment into our hearts— judgment between what is right and wrong without God in the conversation. We don't need God anymore to tell us what is good or bad because we have a measuring tool inside of us. With this new interior knowledge comes a new struggle for all of us to enjoy: spiritual slavery. We are now enslaved in an atmosphere of judgment and division where we all try to compete to the top of our knowledge of good and evil.

Have we ever stopped to ask why the Father didn't want us to have that knowledge? Was it the knowledge itself that was wrong? No, not exactly. It was deeper than that. It was what the knowledge revealed in Eve's heart and what it reveals it in ours: we don't trust God to tell us what is right and wrong. We crave knowledge for ourselves so we can rule ourselves and others with the code of conduct. When our code of conduct is established we can negotiate with it, modify it, and tweak it to serve our purposes. Remember, it was the enemy who was trying to convince our original parents that the Father was withholding something good from them by not letting them have it. The enemy had no comment on the knowledge itself, because that was not the point. He wanted them to take the fruit not only to disobey, but also to agree with him that they could lean on their own understanding. That's why Proverbs 3:5 reminds us to "Trust in the Lord with all your heart and lean not on your own understanding; in all your ways acknowledge him, and he will make your paths straight." The Father had plans to lead us by his own hand from the start because he loves us and wants to be near us. The fall took place not at the bite into the fruit from the tree, but as soon as the original Mom and Dad questioned the intent of God's heart.

Adam and Eve had access to the presence of God. They shared an intimacy with him that others have not known. They walked with him, in person, in the cool of the day. He desired a deep and trusting relationship with them, and, therefore, he wanted them to rely on him for their understanding of the way things in his world really worked because he had, after all, made it. Inside of that kind of trust there would be no need for them to have the knowledge of good and evil, and so all he required was trust. All they gained was blissful intimacy with their Creator. The Father didn't want them to eat the fruit because he wanted them to depend on him, rely on him, and trust him explicitly, which is just what our children do when they are small. That kind of trust is the only way to really know him as Father.

Don't you know the enemy was aware of all of this? So his temptation to them wasn't a temptation to know more, rather it was to trust God less. The enemy knew that with the Spirit of God as our guide to understanding the world around us, we would see more clearly and would have wisdom beyond the natural if we trusted him explicitly. He also knew that eating from the tree of the knowledge of good and evil would not only be the disobedient act that would separate us from God, but also that it would forever challenge us with what that knowledge brought us: measurements, judgements, and comparisons. The separation that came with Adam and Eve's disobedience created a void in our world that this new knowledge could never really overcome—knowledge is no replacement for relationship. We are now cursed with Adam and Eve's intellect, which thinks it can ascend to a height that can satisfy our souls. That soul-satisfaction, however, is reserved exclusively for the kiss of God.

To win us back to his kisses God had to create the ultimate list under which we could die painfully and so realize the foolishness of our attempts at replacing intimacy with judgment. He created the Law of Moses. The people of Moses created the law of the Law of Moses. We, over hundreds of generations, have perfected it into a million-and-one nuanced ways to keep the perfect judgment and life-order. Why are we so good at adding to the laws of right and wrong in our world? It is the curse of the Tree of the Knowledge of Good and Evil. Don't get the idea that God's laws seeded disobedience in our hearts. No. Disobedience was already in our hearts growing in the shade of our own special tree. We were happy to try and embrace the Law then at the foot of Mt. Sinai and we are happy to try it today. I know I was happy to both try and to put the judgment on others as well.

The law is supposed to be like the mirror held up in front of us that says, "This is the perfection that you will never be able to attain, so give up quick and seek God for mercy." I am amazed at humankind's willingness to live under the law of failure and death so consistently and persistently. I am amazed at my own willingness to live in that atmosphere as long as I did. How about you?

I NEED TO BE RIGHT

A CONFESSION

"Triple Breve Espresso Macchiato," I mumbled groggily at the counter.

"Early meeting today?" asked Lindsey, one of my favorite baristas.

"Yeah…she forgot that sleep is a good thing!" I quipped back. About that time Kaitlin walked in the door.

"Why did we have to meet at 7am again?" I asked.

"I'm going out of town, remember? I leave at 10 and I have a bit more packing to do".

"Oh yeah," I replied. She ordered her normal organic soy latte and we sit down for a 30-minute catch up chat.

Kaitlin and I have an interesting history. She's friends with one of my friends from college. We met a few years ago and, shortly thereafter, we made that little connection. Since then we've grown a deep friendship. More recently she has really come online with her need to save the planet and today she's on a rampage. She was slightly appalled that we were at Starbucks to begin with, as for her that somehow represented the evils of corporate America. But she had found a loophole for her own guilt when Lindsey told her about Starbucks' new program to recycle used plastic cups. Whew. I swear, we haven't touched a single topic yet where we don't end up back at solar panels, CFL's, or why I'm not composting. I love her, but...for real...at this point in our relationship I am sincerely annoyed.

My macchiato that morning was so perfect that it distracted me from what Kaitlin was actually saying. However, my ears perked up at the statement that had just left her lips: "I find myself supporting the ideals of Chez Guevere, Fidel Castro, and Hugo Chavez."

No, she didn't, I think to myself, but then I can't contain my incredulity, "What!? You can't be serious Kaitlin! You know they're communists right? They press their people into submission without representation and rule a people that have no voice!"

"Yes, but at least the people are taken care of at the most basic level...food, shelter, health care," she responded. My God, I can't believe that we have created a conversation in our culture that allows that baseline of provision to be a system for approving a governing system.

"I know, I know...I saw Michael Moore's movie, too...but have you ever been to Cuba?" I asked. "Have you seen what communism has done to the souls of the people there?"

And with that our conversation had turned totally political and my face began to heat up. I could feel my fight or flight instincts firing up. I was self-aware enough to ask myself, "What is this about? Why do I unexpectedly want to stand on the table and argue? I love Kaitlin, but now I feel there is something separating us. I find myself not wanting to talk to her anymore. I wonder if she even knows God."

I needed to know why, after all these years and after the restoration of my intimacy with Father God, had I become internally unhinged by the words coming out of Kaitlin's mouth. I wanted to be free to love, but I was powerless to love and instead was compelled to judge. That conversation and that confession of my own weakness in the face of that philosophical argument set me on another journey of self-discovery.

A DEEPER LOOK

I remember Vorina. I mean, who could forget that name. She had hair to her feet, she applied no make-up, and she wore dresses every day. I always admired her adherence to her religious traditions, but wondered if she ever felt trapped. She was a friend in high school that was a part of a Pentacostal church tradition, and secretly I wished to help set her free.

I also think back to Sarah. She was a devout Catholic. We were friends in elementary school, and I remember even then being amazed at how dedicated she was to the special classes she attended, the prayers she prayed, and how she seemed to constantly wonder if God was mad at her. I wondered if I could help her as well.

I also remember a boy who wanted to date me my senior year. (Yes, as you can tell, I was boy crazy. The "why's" behind that problem are for the next book.) He often asked me the same kind of questions I would have asked Vorina. The ones about why I lived by this list of do's and don'ts. He wasn't a Christian, so I told him that although I wanted to make out with him, I definitely couldn't date him. Our arguments back then always came back to how my life seemed so tedious and dull because of my rules and how he was going to go to hell if he didn't become a Christian. I don't think my Christianity inspired him to know God in the least. I guess I was his Vorina. Funny isn't it? An unbeliever had a better take on the spiritual slavery in my life than I—or anyone in my church for that matter—had.

When you are trying to find your sense of O.K.-ness by being right or wrong, your life becomes a series of comparisons and you end up in a self-imposed prison. Life becomes a work camp of sorts. I think "work camp" is the right idea because it sounds like a place where slaves would be at home. Slaves, after all, would feel very out of place in free-land or at family camp. Slaves need stuff to do, stuff to prove, and some people to compare themselves with. This is where religious tradition is a perfectly tailored fit for our slave-shaped souls.

Growing up I began to find myself more and more enslaved in spiritual slavery work camp. I became comfortable with it, and I became good at it. I found out that in work camp you could work to be on the top of the pile and get some attention for it. It wasn't my parents who reinforced the way of slavery in my life as much as it was my religious tradition. My tradition taught me to "be right or get out" and I took its advice. I began to get my feelings of rightness from my performance in work camp, which depended on my always knowing what was right to do or think in any situation. I had to know what was right, otherwise how could I prove I could obey the right rule?

As I stated in an earlier chapter, this behavior was recognized as normal in my religious tradition. Choosing what was right and then following the rule was the very foundation of being a Christian-in-action in my tradition. We could say with our mouths that our salvation was totally because of Jesus' love and that it was a gift, but you could never ever have proved that by watching how we lived, what we talked about, and what made us feel O.K. This is a great lesson between a thing said and a way lived and which one proves the truth about us.

It would be one thing if the measurements ended at theologians and teachers who wrote books, but no, it doesn't stop there. We have an internal awareness that we have lost our way to the rightness we long for. We feel so behind that when we find a law of righteousness, it is our deep instinct to work toward it. It is in our DNA to compare and judge because we ate from the tree of the knowledge of good and evil, and now we use our internal judgment talents to divide ourselves from one another. It was why people outside my religious tradition were as much "them" and not "us" as people who didn't even believe in God. If you believed something different than "us" then you were a "them" and you were not to be trusted. The judgment and division was to keep us safe. Not so much safe from each other, but safe inside our self-righteousness that was based on being right...all the time. If you were ever right and I was ever wrong, then the foundations of my safe-house would have crumbled. May it never be! You must be wrong, so stay over there with "them!" So my life in Jesus was very much an "us vs. them" situation in almost every direction. No wonder I was so difficult to be around.

I remember having dinner at a restaurant after a church service one Sunday night and seeing Vorina and some of her friends who had just come from their service. Somehow we ended up in a conversation about their tradition, Pentecostal, and how we, in my tradition, were missing out on so much because we weren't baptized in the Holy Ghost and didn't speak in tongues. Instead of a possible invitation into a deeper love relationship with Jesus via the Holy Spirit, it turned into a comparison of what they had that we didn't have...and how they were crazy and we were not! Before it was all over we were all in an argument and one guy was pressuring me to be baptized in the Holy Spirit in order to "really be saved." I left in tears. Their pursuit of Jesus and their engagement with the Holy Spirit had become a measuring tool instead of a relationship. Just like my pursuit of Jesus was measured by my list of do's and don'ts and my adequacy without the Holy Spirit.

I guess it is pretty easy to see that this is not what Jesus died for. He did not die so we could be members of a great, historic group squabble that is result of the fruit on the tree of the knowledge of good and evil. He gave his life so we could have something "abundant," and I want to be on my way to that. Do you want to come along?

WHAT I AM LEARNING

Jesus had an encounter with the professionally religious in Mark 7:5-8. This passage reads:

> So the Pharisees and teachers of the law asked Jesus, "Why don't your disciples live according to the tradition of the elders instead of eating their food with 'unclean' hands?"
>
> He replied, "Isaiah was right when he prophesied about you hypocrites; as it is written: 'These people honor me with their lips, but their hearts are far from me. They worship me in vain; their teachings are but rules taught by men.' You have let go of

the commands of God and are holding on to the traditions of men."

Notice that the indictment Jesus weighs against these men was not that they obsessed over ceremonial religious stuff, but that they had let go of God's way and had begun to cling to the traditions of men. They trusted in their grid, their system, their way of doing things to give them safety. They had consumed the fruit of the tree of the knowledge of good and evil and now they were trying to live by it. When people begin to trust and cling to their way of doing religion instead of clinging to the hands of the Father, then the spirit of religion begins to gain power.

What do we mean by the spirit of religion? Well, in common terms, the spirit of a thing is simply the essence of its attitude or disposition. This is why we could say about a rowdy little boy, "He has a spirit of mischief," or about a bitter person, "They have a spirit of anger." In this kind of language I am not assigning a supernatural force to it, but simply stating the nature of that person at that time. However, I think we all understand that if a person maintains their bitterness and anger for a long time, then they will open the door for supernatural partnership with some literal spirits of anger. This kind of partnership takes the manifestation of anger to a whole new level. This kind of invitation can intersect with dark forces in our world, whether we are believers or not. If we maintain an agreement with an addiction, or with unforgiveness, or with judgment, or with sensuality, etc., we will create an opportunity for the devil to add fuel to the fire, so to speak.

Have you ever thought about what the spirit of religion really is? I believe it is the spirit behind slavery and the one which adds the false feelings of spiritual righteousness. It is both the spirit that whispers in the ear of every human saying, "You are not enough...you haven't measured up," and the spirit that says, "If you do these things you will become good in the eyes of God and clear your conscience of failure." It drives us to work to be better, strive to do right things, and it convinces us that in being "right" we are O.K. with God. Jesus dealt with the spirit of religion when he taught against trusting in the traditions of men. The traditions of men that he spoke against was a system of "doing right" that the religious people of his day clung to. We have our own systems today, and they are just as powerful.

To think that the spirit of religion is reserved for organized religions is naive. As humans we were made to worship the Father God as the giver of life and love. This worship was meant to be given out of a heart of thankfulness to God, however, much of our thankfulness is given to inferior things that have gained our affection. We form systems of worship, servitude, and dedication toward whatever makes us feel whole and good. This is the basic formation of religion. As people recognize what gives them a feeling of worth and value, they begin to give it their focus. Worship is a good word for this because it encompasses everything from reverence, to zeal, to the application of life commitments toward whatever fills our void. Over time, those with leadership grace will inevitably write a paper about their object of worship and convince or even bully enough people into agreeing with them, at which point there arises a list of "do's" and "don'ts" to adhere to. Once there is a grid set for worship of something, then guilt and shame naturally fuse to the "don'ts" and pride and honor meld to the "do's." This is the basic stuff of the spirit of religion.

Let's consider some of these unconventional forms of religion. How about social systems? Socialites, as an easy example, must adhere to a way of living, an order for their life, and a list of relationships to associate with and not associate with in order to be acceptable in their families.

How about politics? Depending on where you live and who your friends are, if you vote for the "wrong" party you could face rejection or at least a good lecture on why you are wrong. Whether many of us want to admit it or not, we have put our trust for our sense of well-being inside of our preferred political system. If we disagree, then you are in opposition to my well-being, and therefore we draw lines of "us" and "them" in the sand, creating division and self-righteousness.

How about environmental activists? Have you spent any time with someone who really, aggressively believes that humans are melting the planet? The weight of judgment brought against those who don't agree with them, who don't recycle their trash, or who don't drive a hybrid is palpable. After one solid conversation with a person like this, you will probably be panicked into selling your car, planting some trees, and showering only once a week.

In all of these cases and a hundred more, if you don't obey the acceptable list of "do's" and "dont's" you are judged. This is what humanity does in order to deal with the internal message that says "you don't measure up." We must create a grid with which to measure the world around us so that we can measure up to something. Do you remember how I said earlier that if a person holds on to judgment in their heart long enough that it may invite dark spiritual partnership? Well, the spirits of religion are happy to join into our lives and communities when we hold on to these judgements and when we hold on to anger, unforgiveness, comparisons, divisions, and enslavement to the traditions of men, as well. The spirits of religion are also very happy to keep us inside of church activity and commitments that help us feel righteous but never lead us to intimacy with the Father. Spirits of religion may even be most comfortable inside of official "we have it right and you don't" church communities.

There really are spiritual forces at work to break down our trust relationship with God. They are demonic and they want to destroy our ability to enjoy God. They want to destroy the dreams God has for us. I don't know about you, but I can see that much of my journey has been affected by my choosing to cling to the traditions of men, and I have empowered the enemy to bring destruction in and around my life.

I want that to come to an end.

Much of my journey has been influenced by the spirit of slavery in my heart.

I want that to come to an end.

And, unfortunately, I would have to say that I have at times made partnerships with, or at least temporarily agreed with, the spirits of religion.

I really, really want that partnership to come to an end.

It is time for us to overcome this enslaving need to be right. We must learn to find our rightness in the eyes of God alone. I believe God has a path to freedom laid out before us...will you come along.

I NEED MORE

A CONFESSION

My knuckles were white and my fingers locked around the steering wheel as sheets of rain doused my minivan. I was six hours from home in the middle of Nowhere, New Mexico on my way back from visiting my parents in Texas. My boys were asleep in the seats behind me and I prayed that God would protect me from hydroplaning. Driving in the rain is one of my least favorite things in the world. It's right up there with eating deviled eggs and wearing panty hose.

Driving has been a major component of our ministry life. The first six years of our marriage we toured full-time and fly dates were the exception. I could drive for three hours without a pee break, and I had even perfected my skills at backing up an equipment trailer. With all of those years of road travel under my belt I knew what worked to keep me awake…carrots and talking. Carrots are great road food because they have an unending amount of chew-ability and are easy on the waistline. Talking is superior to music because it makes you think…and often talk back. In this situation (and anytime Ben was napping during our touring years) the talk came from another source besides a human in the passenger's seat. Since sleeping was, as I have mentioned before, my husband's surpassing grace, I had a lot of time on the road to listen to talk radio, teaching tapes, and audio books and to have open conversations with all of them.

On this drive I was listening to one of my favorite teachers of all time, Graham Cooke. Not only does he have wonderful revelation and teaching grace, he also has that lovely British accent that makes him sound even smarter. Listening to Graham always compels me to love the Father more and I am always impressed at the end of the teaching with God's goodness. In this particular recording Graham was telling about a plane ride he was on and a unique exchange he had with the stranger seated next to him.

As he talks, two points begin to weigh heavy in my heart. One came when he started talking about his "testimony." He said that his testimony is not the story of how he got "saved;" instead, his testimony is what God is doing in him now. The second thing that got me was when he relayed a picture of how he usually saw the Father in his mind's eye. In his mind he was always in the Father's lap with the Father's arm around him. Such a beautiful picture. When the tape was over, I turned off the stereo. To the drone of the road noise my mind drifted to these two points. When I thought about my testimony I came up lacking. I couldn't think of much I would talk about in my relationship with God right now. I mean, I was thankful for my family's health, and the provision of a home, and for the things we need. But I knew that I didn't have the kind of testimony that Graham was really talking about. This bothered me and I didn't know what to do about it.

The rain had just subsided and the sun was straight overhead and bouncing off of the mesas that flanked the highway. My eyes squinted even behind sunglasses as I pulled off in Raton to fill up with gas. When I got back on the highway I let my mind float back to the second part that had been so powerful to me: *How do I see the Father when I approach him?*

As I thought about this question I realized that I had never seen his face in my imagination, instead I would see his foot tapping on the floor and his arms crossed in a "where have you been?" kind of way. This, by the way, was an improvement on the pictures I recall from my former years when he was angry and wondering why I hadn't been doing more for him. Now, I didn't like this picture at all. It was extra frustrating because I knew that was not who God really was. I had been coming to an understanding that he didn't need me working for him; rather he just wanted to be near me because he loved me. Yet in these scenes he still had room for displeasure. I was still failing him in my lack and infrequency of nearness. Why could Graham have such a sweet relationship with the Father and so much favor, and I always come up short? Where had I gone wrong? What was I doing or not doing that was causing his displeasure?

A DEEPER LOOK

I suffer from what I like to call the *What's Next? Syndrome*. As a child, I could be going to a party and get so excited about it and get there and not be able to really enjoy it because I was always interested in what was next. Would we get chocolate or vanilla cake at the end? What if I didn't like it? As a teenager, I could be sleeping over at a friend's house who I really liked and instead of enjoying the girl talk and fun stuff I would be consumed with wondering what would happen the next day. As an adult, I could be doing something I really loved like playing music with my husband only to be distracted by the nagging question of where we would go for our day off the next day.

I remember that we didn't have a lot in the way of material things growing up but my parents sacrificed immensely to give us what we had.

I remember my mom telling me and my sister at times that we weren't thankful, and she was right. I see it in my own children now. Dang it.

I think part of it is a result of living in the wealthiest nation in the world and living in the same nation that imports the cheapest stuff ever made. My kids can buy toys for a dollar all day. If they have five dollars they can buy five toys that will all break within an hour an a half. The resulting mentality in both my children and in me is this: "Oh well, I'll just buy a new one." I don't think it is good for our souls.

I think that my own lack of thankfulness keeps me from seeing the Father's activity in my life, especially his activity in the present. I didn't, and sometimes still don't, notice the gift of right now because I was always looking to buy my next cheap plastic toy, metaphorically speaking. As I became older I still often felt parched or lonely, and I didn't have eyes to recognize blessings when they came my way. I missed the goodness and the salvation of the Lord even though they were there all the time. I think it is part of why I couldn't recognize what he was doing for me everyday—why I didn't feel I had a real-time testimony.

Are slaves thankful? I guess they are thankful for what they do get— basic shelter and some food. But I wonder if they constantly need to be reminded of what they should be thankful for since nothing seems all that amazing when you are constantly working for the next thing. At my house we have a motto: "You get what you get and you don't throw a fit." This keeps me, the mom, from becoming a short order cook at dinner time.

This saying is a basic motto for slaves as well. It was for me. In the depths of my spiritual slavery I was thankful that I was not going to hell, and for Christ's death that saved me from that, and maybe for my basic provisions. But my What's Next Syndrome was a sign that I was still lacking an understanding of the Father's goodness to me and that I needed a more thankful heart. My problem with slavery prevented me from really receiving his goodness because I couldn't receive his love. And I couldn't receive his love because I was working for it, and his love cannot be earned.

WHAT I AM LEARNING

What our heavenly Father gives us is more than we could ever dream or ask for, and his provision for us as his sons is lavish and plentiful. There is so much language in the Bible that points to his amazing, generous love over his family. Like when Jesus promises in Luke 6:38, "Give, and it will be given to you. A good measure, pressed down, shaken together and running over, will be poured into your lap. For with the measure you use, it will be measured to you."

And in Luke 11:13: "If you then, though you are evil, know how to give good gifts to your children, how much more will your Father in heaven give the Holy Spirit to those who ask him!"

Later in Luke 12:24, Jesus tries to lift our imaginations even further when he speaks of our value to God. He says, "Consider the ravens: They do not sow or reap, they have no storeroom or barn; yet God feeds them. And how much more valuable you are than birds!" In verse 28, he promises our provision: "If that is how God clothes the grass of the field, which is here today, and tomorrow is thrown into the fire, how much more will he clothe you, O you of little faith!"

Not only do we get the basics, but Romans 5:17 proclaims this over us: "For if, by the trespass of the one man, death reigned through that one man, how much more will those who receive God's abundant provision of grace and of the gift of righteousness reign in life through the one man, Jesus Christ."

I want to be able to see God's generosity toward me when it comes. I don't want to live out Jeremiah 17:5-7a, "This is what the Lord says: 'Cursed is the one who trusts in man, who depends on flesh for his strength and whose heart turns away from the Lord. He will be like a bush in the wastelands; he will not see prosperity when it comes. He will dwell in the parched places of the desert, in a salt land where no one lives.'" I don't want to trust in man. I don't want to live constantly striving for the "more" that is around the corner. I must overcome the What's Next Syndrome in order to truly see and be thankful for his present work in my life. I am going to have to learn to depend on him and not on my works, or the my arm of my flesh, for my strength.

I think we can learn to do this together.

Jeremiah 17:7-8 goes on to carve this truth into our hearts: "But blessed is the man who trusts in the Lord, whose confidence is in him. He will be like a tree planted by the water that sends out its roots by the stream. It does not fear when heat comes; its leaves are always green. It has no worries in a year of drought and never fails to bear fruit."

Yes!

Now, that is where I want to be. I want to trust in the Lord and live in constant blessing. I see nothing in his Word except the promises that I most certainly can live in that blessing through my relationship with Jesus. I will put my confidence in him. I do not need the "more" just around the corner that my flesh hopes for. I will not trust in my own works, my own knowledge, or the provisions of men. I will trust in God.

We are going to need some help to learn to trust in God.

In the next section of this book we are going to look into the depth of the help that God himself has provided for us. Are you ready to receive God's help to overcome your orphanhood? Are you ready to be truly free from the spiritual slavery and the spirit of religion? Let's discover his plan together in the next section titled, "A More Beautiful God."

PART 2:
A MORE BEAUTIFUL GOD

RECEIVING THE FATHER'S LOVE

RECEIVE THE FATHER'S LOVE

There were two messages seeded into the heart of mankind in the garden: "You are an orphan who has no Father" and "You are a slave who must work to prove you are worthy of love."

The ability to receive love is crucial to our life as sons, and these messages of orphanism and slavery have impaired our ability to receive the Father's love. This is the core of the relational damage that was done in the garden. Between the lies that speak through our experiences that say we have no Father and the knowledge of good and evil that judges him to be acceptable or not, we have a difficult time accepting the very love we were made for. Do you see this? The enemy wasn't just trying to lure more souls to join him in hell by tempting Adam and Eve. He wasn't just introducing sin to the world to create a division between man and God. He was trying to derail the whole thing! He was trying to derail God's whole plan to love a people that he had made for himself. He hates that God adores us, and so he hates us, the object of God's love, and wants so badly to separate us from the love that God has for us.

But we know he cannot do it. As Romans 8:38-39 says, "For I am convinced that neither death nor life, neither angels nor demons, neither the present nor the future, nor any powers, neither height nor depth, nor anything else in all creation, will be able to separate us from the love of God that is in Christ Jesus our Lord."

Since he doesn't have the power to separate us from the love of God, what does he do in order to keep us in bondage? He works to prevent us from being able to receive the love of the Father. No matter how much love is poured out on us, if our hearts don't believe the truth of who the Father is and the truth of who we are, our hearts will be waxed to his love…and we will suffer almost as if we were separated from it.

Receiving God's love is the foundation of our sonship. We live like sons when we receive the truth of who he is and his love for us into the core of our beings. My friend Judi describes this core as our "love well." She says that our love well has a crack in it due to sin and the fall of mankind. The love of God is the only thing to seal up this crack in our love well. If we try to put the love of others into our well without the love of God being received first, the love of others will slowly seep out. But if we receive his love first, then the imperfect love of others will have a place to rest. We will receive their love and have love overflowing to share with others. When we can't receive the perfect love of the Father , however, we are even more deficient at receiving the imperfect love of others.

You know what it's like to be around someone whose love well is seeping. You can do things for them, compliment them, and care for them, only to find out the next time that you're with them that you have failed them in some way. It seems that you are always behind in your relationship. They desperately need to receive the perfect love of the Father. If they did, then your imperfect attempts to love them would rest in a thankful place in their souls.

So if receiving love is the key to our sonship then how does he convince us of the lies that wax us from the Father's love? Well, remember that because of the fall the soil in the heart of all mankind is ready to receive these lies about the Father. So all the enemy has to do is line up damaging circumstances in our lives that echo those lies and most of his dirty work is done. And on top of it all, these offenses are usually committed by people we trust, so we believe the messages and lies that are communicated in those circumstances even more wholly than we would otherwise.

Do you see the scheme of the enemy now? Our enemy has been trying to deceive us by keeping the truth hidden from view. We were created to receive the Father's love. It is time to discover why we don't trust the Father. It is time to receive healing. We all need to receive the love of the Father. We need to believe and receive the goodness of his character. We need to trust him and have confidence in who he is despite what circumstance and experience the reason of our knowledge of good and evil might tell us about it. It is time to offer forgiveness and let our faith rest solidly in him. Our Father IS love and he wants us to come home. Receive his adoption and let him heal our hearts.

"Father, as we enter this pathway to recovery, help us commit to unlock these mysteries in our own hearts as to why we can't receive your love."

RECEIVE YOUR SONSHIP

Sonship is our destiny. It is offered to all of mankind. We want to be loved and received for who we are. We all want to be loved unconditionally without performance or work. Isn't it good that the Father made a way for us all to experience the answer to these deep desires?

As we saw earlier, the way that he and his very own Son made for us is a painful one. Our salvation begins by confessing our inadequacy and our offenses toward him as sin and then believing in Christ and his perfection in his death and resurrection, but it doesn't end there. That is only the beginning. We were saved to something and that something is the Kingdom of God. His kingdom rules for ever and ever. Our citizenship was purchased by the blood of Jesus and we are labeled sons and daughters, not servants, slaves, or orphans. And it is just the beginning of the abundant life we were created for. Our sonship is the foundation that the rest of our dreams, desires and joys are meant to rest on. We will not be able to rest in the destiny that we have in God on a foundation constructed of anything less than sonship. He didn't save us to be orphans or slaves. Therefore, without faith to believe past the old mindsets that our old DNA gave us we will never please God. I didn't just make that up…it's in Hebrews 11:6. Okay, I added the part about DNA and our old mindsets, but faith is what it takes to move past those ways of living.

You can't think your way out of orphanhood. Sure, you can change some ways of thinking or doing. But without faith, those changes won't stick. It's the same with slavery. You can undo some of what you do, and even do some of your dont's, but breaking your rules won't make you less of a slave and more of a son. It will most likely just make you feel bad later. Instead, it's all about faith. And you can't manipulate or sweat out faith.

Faith is trust.

We can only trust who we believe to be trustworthy.

This is our journey toward God; it is a journey of growing in trust.

This is our quest together. We are finding our pathway to recovery, our pathway to the truth. I am broken and have had a difficult journey to my sonship, but I am not alone. You are just like me. You too have an unfortunate birthmark in the shape of a target on your bum. It is on all of us who are God's beloved and created in his image. The enemy marked us all in the garden. Our DNA code carries the lies of orphanhood and slavery and Jesus is our only hope to be free of them and at home with the Father.

So let's move on! Let's recognize the obstacles that stand between us and our sonship, the clutter in our minds and the lies in our hearts that speak against our acceptance in the Father's heart as his beloved sons and daughters.

I have news for you: You are already your Father's favorite son!

You remember the most quoted parable in the whole New Testament, the Parable of the Prodigal Son in Luke 15. You know, the son who left home and then realized he had made a mistake. It says in verse 20, "So he got up and went to his father. But while he was still a long way off, his father saw him and was filled with compassion for him; he ran to his son, threw his arms around him and kissed him."

These are kisses of affection the Father has for us as well. Yes, the Father has many sons, but when he looks at you, you are his absolute favorite. To be his favorite is to live in his ultimate approval and love at all times. That is where you are because of the miracle of transformation that Jesus has brought to you. Let's look deep into that miracle in the next chapter.

First, let's pray together: "Father, as we begin on this pathway to recovery, help us not to lose heart and shrink back from our destiny as sons and daughters. Give us the strength to press on toward a life lived in the truth of who you made us to be: your favorite!"

RECEIVING THE WORK OF JESUS

A THANKFUL HEART

I want to warm up your heart for this section by inspiring your thankful heart. A thankful heart has creative and restorative power. Psalm 50:23 says: "He who sacrifices thank offerings honors me, and he prepares the way so that I may show him the salvation of God." When I stir up your thankfulness it will make a way for God to literally come closer to you and touch your life.

I remember hearing a story about a priest who was doing work in an impoverished nation. He witnessed people being healed and even raised from the dead amongst the believers there. It was the most amazing expression of miracles he had ever seen. He was pondering why he in all of his years in ministry and experiences with so many believers had never seen such miracles.

While he was there he contracted a deadly disease and was given only a short time to live. He was laying on a bed in the clinic and crying out to the Father. "Why have you done this to me? I am here to help these people and now you are going to let me die, away from my wife and family. Why won't you heal me?" There was no answer. The next day the old woman who had been caring for him daily came into the room. When he saw her he heard the Father say, "Have you thanked me for her? She has been here everyday, dressing your wounds, cleaning up after you, but you have not offered a word of thanks." The priest repented. As he asked the Father to forgive him for his selfishness, the Holy Spirit opened his eyes to the fact that in the midst of their deep poverty, these people were thankful to God for everything. The Father spoke to him and said, "You live in abundance and want for little, yet you have forgotten where what you have comes from. You have not remembered that it all comes from my hand." The priest wept and continued to repent in his heart from the pride that had seated itself in place of thankfulness. He began to thank the Lord for every little thing he could think of. As he did he began to feel a restoring not only of his soul, but of his body as well. The next day he awoke to find that his body was completely healed. A thankful heart had prepared a way for God to bring salvation to his body.

Thankfulness recognizes the true character of God and receives it as goodness. Did you hear that? It receives his goodness and trusts in it. How can we have faith if we do not believe he is good, and how can we believe he is good if we have not noticed his goodness in our lives and thanked him for it?

What is the greatest goodness of all?

The Good News—the Gospel! The Good News that our Father sent us a rescuer and his name is Jesus. He sent his Son not just to teach or offer a healing hand, but to make the ultimate sacrifice of love for each of us. The Father's love was shown to us in the most extravagant display when he placed his only Son on a cross and allowed his innocent hands to be nailed to the beams of wood and his body then dropped into a hole in the ground. Jesus hung there naked and exposed and he took it all on himself...the murder and hatred, the rape and molestation, the anger and bitterness, the sickness and brokenness, every kind of wickedness. And finally, he took on death. He did it because he loves us, and he knew we could never bear the weight of our rebellion against his Father! He wanted to bring us back into the family of God. He did it because he knew that true life is found in the Father's love for us. Jesus knows that what we lost in the garden was communion with our Dad, intimacy with the one who made us and knows us like no one else. The Father wants us to be his sons just like Jesus is his Son.

Let's stop for a moment and say aloud, "Father, I am thankful that you love me so much. I am thankful, Jesus, that you gave yourself completely to me in your love. I receive your love and your work on the cross. Thank you."

I RECEIVE THE WORK OF THE CROSS

I know that many of you reading this book are already believers and have maybe known Jesus for years, even decades. But I won't assume this is true of every reader. Truly, to move on to the next steps in the journey without first receiving the work of the cross could literally make you stumble and fall.

If you have never chosen to submit your whole life to the loving care and total control of Jesus Christ, then it is your first step to becoming a son. Jesus came to give you a way to return home to Dad, Father God, and be received as a son. He gave up his life on the cross and took all of your brokenness, guilt and shame on himself.

To become a child of God, first recognize that your sin, your pride, and your independence has separated you from God, just as it separated Adam and Eve in the garden. Second, repent—totally turn the opposite direction in your heart from the way you have seen God, received his love, and tried to live life on your own. And third, receive his love for you as a son or daughter.

Are you ready to confess to God your need for him and your desire to submit your life to him completely and receive the salvation that Jesus purchased for you? If so, then you can pray this prayer:

Father, I know that my sin and brokenness has separated me from you. I am so sorry for rejecting you, for turning my back from you, and for going my own way. I choose right now to repent and turn away from living my life without you. I want to see you for who you really are. I choose today to receive the death and resurrection of Jesus as my only way to you and to becoming your son/daughter. Thank you for suffering so that I can be with you again. I love you and I choose to receive your love. I pray all of these things in the name of Jesus Christ.

If you just prayed that prayer for the first time, then you have just come into the family of God! You have been born again and you have a new life ahead of you.

I RECEIVE MY RIGHTNESS FROM JESUS

Do you remember who Satan was before he left heaven? He was a beautiful angel. Ezekiel 28 describes him as "the model of perfection, full of wisdom and perfect in beauty." In verse 17 we see what happened to him, though: "Your heart became proud on account of your beauty, and you corrupted your wisdom because of your splendor. So I threw you to the earth." Look at what happened to him. He was cast down from heaven and the presence of God because of his pride—his fascination and love for his own wisdom, and his own beauty. So what does he do to God's beloved creation the first chance he gets? He tempts them to follow in the same steps to destruction that he took. He entices them to believe they can be like God and glory in the knowledge they can attain. Have you ever heard the saying, "misery loves company?" Well, it's true for Satan. He really wants us to keep him company!

If you know someone who is always negative, you have probably noticed that it doesn't take long for them to lure others into the same "woe is me" world view. A negative world view desperately needs friends to join in and give it life. Gossip operates much the same way because it reflects the same negative view of others. Gossip loves company, too, and needs a listening ear to accomplish its work. Proverbs 16:28 says, "A perverse man stirs up dissension, and a gossip separates close friends." When we take a look at Satan's plan to bring harm to us we realize he started with some simple gossip. The evil behind his question to Eve in Genesis 1, "Did God say?" was the questioning of God's character. It was nothing more than character attacking gossip. The enemy's desire to lure humanity into sharing his destiny began inside of this gossip that questioned the character of God and his ultimate love for mankind, and it ends by helping people believe that they can do better than to trust in God. By fabricating a sense of God-likeness in a person's mind and reinforcing it with a faulty knowledge of good and evil Satan has accomplished a very effective attack on our ability to trust in God.

And trusting God is the key to everything, isn't it?

In the New Testament, the Apostle Paul spends much of his writing bringing correction to many of the believers, especially in Galatia, who also had trouble trusting God. He starts his letter to them by saying "Grace and peace to you," but the very next sentence is "I'm astonished at how quickly you are turning to a new gospel." What was this new gospel? It was a gospel of working to keep laws and rules and, ultimately, to please men. This showed they did not trust God, but they did trust in in their own faulty knowledge. The Galatians were coming up against what we wrestle with consistently from our old DNA: slavery.

Paul knew that as immature believers the Galatians were weak and could easily fall back into the old slave-way of living. He says, "Formerly, when you did not know God, you were *slaves* to those who by nature are not gods. But now that you know God—or rather are known by God— how is it that you are turning back to those weak and miserable principles? Do you wish to be *enslaved* by them all over again? You are observing special days and months and seasons and years!" (Galatians 3:28-4:10)

Paul was concerned that these believers were reverting to immaturity by returning to the bondage of the basic principles of the world. Do you see he's talking about those principles that the Galatians had previously used to judge good from evil? The Galatians were trusting in their own ability to follow rules to make them worthy of Christ. Do you see that it isn't any different than how we live? Our need to follow rules, do's, and don'ts, in order to be accepted in our traditions? This is living under the spirit of slavery.

These basic principles are also ways that we can trade in knowledge, trade in strength, or trade in any other value system that might give us a sense of position in the spiritual or social scene. By *trade* I mean establishing our value by using these inferior things to gain favor and position with others. It is as though we are buying and selling our abilities to one another in order to move up in the world. It is the knowledge of good and evil, coupled with this trading, that emboldens us to justify stepping on the heads of others to get what we want, whether that's a position or a place of respect or leadership or honor.

These principles leave us in bondage to the mindset that says to our hearts, "You must work to be loved. You must be approved before you can be accepted." It is the dark thread that leads us away from the Father's heart and makes us believe that we must work to receive his love. And if we have to work for his love, it is not his unconditional love we are receiving. And if we have to work to receive his perfect love, then we have to work all the more to receive love from others. This is barely living at all.

Do you remember the story about Jesus being at the house of two sisters in Luke 10? One was busy making food, preparing a table, and serving the guests. The other, Mary, was sitting at his feet listening to him talk. Can you see the picture? Martha pokes her head around the corner and says, "Jesus, aren't you going to make Mary help me or do I have to do all the work alone?" I love his reply (I hear it in my own heart sometimes): "Martha, you are worried and upset about many things but only one thing is needed. Mary has chosen what is better, and it will not be taken away from her" (Luke 10:41-42). Oh, can you hear Martha make a "hmph" sound and march off to do more work? Martha struggled under the spirit of slavery. Mary was free to trust and free to love. The better way is the way of trust and love—trusting the Father and receiving his love.

When we question the integrity of the Father and then subsequently put our trust in our own abilities, we have fallen from grace. In Galatians 5:4 Paul says, "You who are trying to be justified by law have been alienated from Christ; you have fallen away from grace." Here, he challenges them to stop following the law and start overcoming the spirit of religion. He wanted them to live by faith and not cling to their own works. He wanted them to cling to God and see that their right standing in this life comes solely by trusting in Jesus.

When the spirits of religion enter into our commitments we become enslaved by the spirit of religion. Here is what Paul has to say to us about what happens when we live by the law instead the promise:

> For through the law I died to the law so that I might live for God. I have been crucified with Christ and I no longer live, but Christ lives in me. The life I live in the body, I live by faith in the Son of God, who loved me and gave himself for me. I do not set aside the grace of God, for if righteousness could be gained through the law, Christ died for nothing! You foolish Galatians! Who has bewitched you? Before your very eyes Jesus Christ was clearly portrayed as crucified. I would like to learn just one thing from you: Did you receive the Spirit by observing the law, or by believing what you heard? Are you so foolish? After beginning with the Spirit, are you now trying to attain your goal by human effort? (Galatians 2:19–3:3)

Whoa! Paul is really giving it to them! I think it must have really bothered him to see them putting their trust in the law and their rules to lead them instead of trusting in the Spirit of God. They weren't being wicked; do you see that? They were simply choosing to trust in their knowledge of good and evil in their measurement of things instead of being led by the Holy Spirit. And look what he asks them: "who has bewitched you?" In other words, who has put you under a curse? They were subjecting themselves to a curse by serving a law of approval and rightness that had nothing to do with trusting the Father. By living like that they were throwing Jesus' life and work under the bus, as it were, and enslaving themselves to the spirits of religion.

In John 8:34 Jesus says, "everyone who commits a sin is a slave to sin." He goes on to draw the contrast between slaves and sons in the next verse. He says, "a slave has no permanent place in the family, but a son belongs to it forever." In Galatians 3:28, Paul expands this topic even further. He begins by flattening the playing field: "There is neither Jew nor Greek, there is neither slave nor free man, there is neither male nor female; for you are all one in Christ Jesus. And if you belong to Christ, then you are Abraham's descendants, heirs according to promise." He says this to emphasize that division does not belong in the family of sons. Division belongs to slaves. The spirit of slavery/religion want us to prefer ourselves over one another in order to feel O.K. We are not made right by anything we do or think; rather, we are made right by the gift of Jesus to us—his own righteousness that he has shared.

"Thank you, Jesus, I receive my rightness from you alone."

I RECEIVE MY ADOPTION

Paul continues in Galatians 4, "So also we, when we were children, we were in slavery under the basic principles of the world. But when the time had fully come, God sent his Son, born of a woman, born under Law, to redeem those under Law, that we might receive the full rights of sons" (Galatians 4:3-5). You can see now that our pathway to recovery was forecasted.

It is the pathway of freedom.

It is the pathway of adoption.

Paul is shouting out this truth now that adoption into God's family is the key to overcoming the spirit of slavery, just as it is the key to overcoming the spirit of orphanhood. And then to the crescendo of these beautiful thoughts that Paul has for us he adds, "Because you are sons, God sent the Spirit of his Son into our hearts, the Spirit who calls out, 'Abba, Father.' So you are no longer a slave, but a son; and since you are a son, God has made you also an heir" (Galatians 4:6-7).

This is our destiny in the work of Jesus. He has shared his sonship with us. We are even joint heirs with him in the Kingdom of God. Amazing. True. We can never turn back to trying to earn our way into the presence of God. How foolish it would be to try and earn what God has so freely given in the gift of his Son to us. He has given us our new place as sons at his table, and he has bestowed on us a kingdom that is populated only with sons. As Jesus confirms in Luke 22:29, "And I confer on you a kingdom, just as my Father conferred one on me."

It is our destiny to be known by him. And the only way to be known by him is to be vulnerable and the only way to be vulnerable is to open our hearts and trust. 1 Corinthians 8:3 says that "the man who loves God is known by God." So we see that love and trust go hand in hand. If we are to know in our hearts that we are children of the Most High God—fully adopted heirs of his kingdom—then we must learn to trust him.

I RECEIVE THE MIND OF CHRIST

I believe it is the Father who gives us every good gift (James 1:17). And I also believe that the gifts that are within each of us are not only given from his hand but are also woven into us from within himself (Psalm 139:15-16). He finds great pleasure in weaving these gifts and capacities and dreams into every one of us, and he loves the process of us discovering each of them along the journey of our lives. The problem for us is that our orphanhood gets in the way of the simple delight of what is within us and makes those things into our identities. Remember, orphans are looking so hard to find their own gifts in order to establish their identities that they fail to see that they are gifts themselves.

The lie that the enemy seeks to sow into our hearts, that we have no Father, leads us to find our sense of adequacy from external sources. Those are often people's opinions of us or positions of influence that we can attain. The problem with finding our identity in what we do is that as soon as what we do changes or morphs or goes away, we're lost again, which means that in our cores we are still living like orphans who don't really know who our Father is and therefore we don't really know who we are.

This is where the enemy can lure us if we are not secure in our identity as sons and daughters in the Father. Our identities are meant to be in the Father and not in the gifts he gave us. Instead, those gifts are meant to be tools to love people with and they are meant to bring delight to our own hearts. They were not meant to define us, give us our worth, or tell us who we are. If our worth is constantly being determined by our place in the world or determined by our gifts then we must always progress. We must constantly achieve and improve and become more and more excellent. And if we are to be more excellent, then we will try to be better than the next guy, which means that our focus is on ourselves and the next guy and not on the Father. It also means that competition and getting ahead become internally endorsed as a means to an end. And it means that any casualties suffered because of those means are justified because we become "someone" as a result.

But listen to this: "Since, then, you have been raised with Christ, set your hearts on things above, where Christ is seated at the right hand of God. Set your minds on things above, not on earthly things. For you died, and your life is now hidden with Christ in God" (Colossians 3:1-3). Paul outlines here that when we are not seeing ourselves as sons of the Father, hidden in Christ, we are tempted with things from our earthly nature. Things like sexual immorality, impurity, lust, evil desires and greed, anger, rage, malice, slander, and filthy language often seem like tools to help us find a place in this world when we are lost orphans (Col. 3:5). These things, however, are quickly discovered to be the tools of broken relationships. They destroy relationships. They divide us. They keep us from loving one another. This is how we understand what *sin* really is: it is the stuff that keeps us from receiving and giving love well.

When our sense of worth, value and general okay-ness comes from what we do, we naturally take our eyes off of Christ and put them on our achievements, giving way to envy, jealousy and selfish ambition. James is in agreement with Paul when he says, "For where you have envy and selfish ambition, there you find disorder and every evil practice" (James 3:16).

How about that? Every evil practice comes as a natural by-product of envy and selfish ambition. And envy and selfish ambition come from a need to find our identity in what we do instead of in who we are in the Father. And our need to find our identity in what we do instead of in who we are in the Father is a natural by-product of looking for a place or position. Can you see how division and brokenness in the family of God is not simply a result of differing opinions or theology but instead a direct result of a people who are trying to answer their own questions of identity? It's the evidence that we struggle to understand who our Father is and that he wants to be with us, that he wants to claim us as his own children and put his hands of approval on us and say, "I love you because you are mine, not because of what you do."

When we receive the mind of Christ, we no longer need to strive for anything because we know that as God's favorite sons we already have it all! Everything we need is ours, and all that we have ever dreamed or will dream of is all coming true in our place with God.

RECEIVING THE HOLY SPIRIT

THE TRANSFORMING POWER

The Holy Spirit has come to lead us into our sonship by speaking the truth in us and to us. It is not simply believing in Jesus as the Christ and trusting his death and resurrection that brings us into our sonship. It is by the transforming work of the Holy Spirit that we receive that understanding. That's right. I said it. Unless we receive the help of the Holy Spirit in an ongoing daily way, we will never have victory and walk with confidence in our sonship. We must be transformed from children who live like slaves to sons who understand and live into their adoption and inheritance in God. We desperately need supernatural, ongoing, right-here kind of help.

As I mentioned earlier in the book, I grew up in a doctrinal tradition that didn't embrace the work of the Holy Spirit. On the contrary, there was often teaching directly against the idea of being "filled with" or "baptized by" the Holy Spirit. It was understood that we got all of the Holy Spirit we needed when we were saved. As a result, I never really gave much thought to the Holy Spirit until later in my life. I just accepted what was taught without question. I realize now that this teaching is widespread and widely accepted, and while I'm not trying to stir up a revolt, I would like to present some questions to you that I began to ask myself. So here goes…

OVERCOMING HOLY SPIRIT MYTHS:

Myth #1
The Trinity is a buffet:
take only the parts you want.

I've heard this one quite a bit: The Holy Spirit is the loose canon of the Trinity. He makes people do things they don't want to do and he can easily be manipulated by immature believers who need attention. He is optional, like the chocolate pudding at a Chinese buffet. You need Jesus to save you and you need the Father to be…well, the Father…but the Holy Spirit? Well, what does he really do, anyway? We got the Holy Spirit in a package deal and we shouldn't try to press the issue any further.

I can understand the mechanics of this logic if I filter it through my slave mindset: We are here to follow the rules and get the work done that is required in order for us to be acceptable to the Father, right? So if the Holy Spirit is mostly touchy-feely and is not accomplishing salvation or being our Father, then what is he doing besides causing controversy?

It would probably be better to just leave him alone. Maybe if we leave him alone, he'll leave us alone."

Myth #2
The power of the Holy Spirit can be abused by immature believers.

This is something I heard growing up in my religious tradition: Beware, the power of the Holy Spirit can be abused by zealous, young believers.

Now let me ask you, if he is supernatural, how can we abuse him? Really, think about it. If he's a part of the Trinity, then he's part of God. Is God really so impotent that we can abuse his power and use it to take advantage of others? No, of course not. So it follows that it must be him who is taking advantage of those he occupies. Well, that doesn't make any sense either.

Hmm.

Maybe people are just acting out in their brokenness, their orphanhood, their slavery? And maybe they (and we) just blamed their brokenness on the work of the Holy Spirit?

Myth #3
The Holy Spirit will make us weird.

Being seen as culturally unacceptable is usually unsavory to most believers, so the thought that the Holy Spirit might do something we don't want or like is threatening. Some have taken the "weird" quotient as part of their identity, however, and have run it at full throttle.

But other believers say that the Holy Spirit is a gentleman and won't do things to you that you don't want him to do. Well, that puts fears of being embarrassed to rest momentarily, but let's remember the Holy Spirit is one of the God-head. This is the same God-head who spat in the dirt and made mud to heal the eyes of the blind man through Jesus. I don't think a gentleman would wipe spit-dirt on anyone's eyes. This same God made Zechariah mute for nine months just because he asked how his wife, who was well along in years as the story goes, could become pregnant. That was not very nice or gentleman-like. And this is the same Holy Spirit that when poured out on the disciples (who had been waiting in the upper room as instructed by Jesus, mind you) made them appear to be drunk...all stumbling around acting sloshed...while they were trying to tell people about Jesus. So much for the Holy Spirit being a gentleman. He must have higher plans.

His disrespect toward our sense of propriety reminds me of the moment in the movie adaptation of C.S. Lewis' book, *The Lion, the Witch, and the Wardrobe*, when Tumnus speaks of Aslan as a fierce, wild, and untamed lion. To this Lucy replies, "but he is good." Our God is not tame. The Father's love could not be tamed by the enemy, and so, in a dramatic act, he crushed his only Son with the weight of the world's wickedness. Jesus' love for us could not be tamed; instead, it made him a spectacle for us on the cross. The Holy Spirit equally cannot be tamed, and he does the unseen work of drawing our hearts to repentance, teaching us about our sonship, healing the sick, raising the dead, and communing with us spirit to spirit in other tongues. But, he is good.

Myth #4
We got all we needed at salvation.

What about the idea that we got all of the Holy Spirit when we were saved? If this is the case then we have to disregard the words of Jesus when he told the disciples that they were going to be baptized with the Holy Spirit. Some have said that that was just for the disciples so they could begin the work of spreading the Gospel. But Peter struggles with the same question and sees that this is not the case in Acts:

> As I began to speak, the Holy Spirit came on them as he had come on us at the beginning. Then I remembered what the Lord had said, "John baptized with water, but you will be baptized with the Holy Spirit." So if God gave them the same gift as he gave us, who believed in the Lord Jesus Christ, who was I to think that I could oppose God? (Acts 11:15-16)

Later we are encouraged in Ephesians that there is one baptism. I have wondered if that meant only the baptism into Jesus Christ. But Paul says, "For we were all baptized by one Spirit into one body—

whether Jews or Greeks, slave or free—and we were all given the one Spirit to drink" (1 Corinthians 12:13).

Finally, when Jesus was talking to the disciples in John 14:16-18 and 20 about the Holy Spirit he says, "But you know him, for he lives with you and will be in you." Note that Jesus said the Holy Spirit lives *with* the disciples; this was before the day of Pentecost when the power of the Spirit rested on the disciples and was *in* them. So believing in Jesus allowed the Holy Spirit to be with them, but being baptized in the Holy Spirit didn't come until they waited for him at Pentecost.

Myth #5
The Trinity: three for the price of one.

Then there is the idea that the Trinity is a package deal. Well, all three are definitely one and united together. And, indeed, coming to one of them introduces you to all of them, but it doesn't mean that you are friends with all of them. It was Jesus that introduced the idea of us becoming friends, right? Friendship comes to us because Jesus lets us in on his Father's business, right? Jesus said, "I no longer call you servants, because a servant does not know his master's business. Instead, I have called you friends, for everything that I learned from my Father I have made known to you" (John 15:15). So don't you want to be friends with the Holy Spirit as well?

Myth #6
The gift of tongues: a take it or leave it option.

What about tongues? It always seemed so weird to me that the disciples would pray for people to be baptized in the Holy Spirit and then those people would speak in tongues. This was the last piece of the Holy Spirit for me to embrace. I always wanted to leave it out like…yeah, you can be filled, but it doesn't matter if you speak in tongues or not.

Well, I've come to a different conclusion. I will tell you why. First of all, we were made in a secret place, in the depths of the earth like Psalm 139 says. Was that in God's underground baby making lair? Or was it a poetic way for the psalmist to suggest we were formed in the spirit realm. And if when we pass from this natural state to eternity we are spirit, then isn't it possible we will speak a spirit language? We came from the realm of spirit and we will continue on in the same realm. So could we consider that a spirit language is a native tongue for us? I understand that a notion like this could really wig some people out, but it's just a question to get us started.

Second, I believe that the whole idea of a baptism in the Spirit and speaking in tongues is our choice to submit our intellect and the knowledge of good and evil to the Father completely. When you embrace the Holy Spirit, get baptized, become best buds—however you want to say it—you are accepting something other-worldly. It can not be explained by your natural mind, your knowledge can't even grasp it completely, much less explain all that he is. It is utterly offensive to our natural minds, to the knowledge of man, and to the pattern of this world. So the movement of your lips in an unknown language is like your flesh agreeing with your spirit that you are willing to submit your mind, your reason, and your intellect to the power and presence of the Holy Spirit completely.

Lastly, the idea that your prayer language, (and, by the way, this is what I'm speaking of here, not the gift of tongues as described in 2 Corinthians which requires a translation), has to overcome you and come out of your mouth involuntarily is a misconception. It is possible for that to happen, but it is not the way that it will happen for all. Think about it. We don't require this kind of possession from other gifts that the Spirit inspires.

Consider teaching, for instance. Often when I'm teaching I feel the presence of the Lord in my physical body and I know that he is inspiring my words...it is really cool. But at that point did he take over my mouth? No. Sometimes when I am praying for a friend and moving my own mouth to say words that I think of, I sense the presence of the Lord and will know again that he is inspiring my words. Again, did I go auto-lips for Jesus on that one? No.

It is the same with my prayer language, or speaking in tongues. I prayed to receive the Holy Spirit multiple times under the misconception that I would speak unprovoked in another language. It wasn't until a couple of years later that a friend encouraged me just to try it. I thought that was so weird. But, because it was just she and I (and she was weird, too) I gave it a try. You know what? It was just like teaching or praying. I began making gibberish with my mouth, pressing right past that super awkward feeling of being a complete dork and then I felt the presence of the Lord. I had to keep doing it over a few weeks, practicing everyday, before it stopped feeling like I was just making up stuff.

Now I can attest to the purpose that Paul gives for tongues in 1 Corinthians 14:4. It edifies and builds up my spirit man. When I need to hear the Father, the first thing I do is pray in the spirit. In doing so, I'm often inspired by the Holy Spirit of a specific thing to pray, or a picture or a scripture will come to mind relating to what I'm praying for. Could I hear the Lord before I asked to be filled with the Spirit or before I submitted my intellect to the nuttiness of tongues? Sure, I could hear his still, small voice. But once I chose to agree that I didn't have to mentally understand everything and I surrendered my knowledge to his supremacy, it's like I plugged into something! I hear his voice even clearer. I see things by the Spirit I never saw before. I comprehend scripture in depths of revelation that I never had previously. It's like I went nuclear!

I RECEIVE BY FAITH, NOT BY SIGHT

My quest for answers also taught me not to be angry at the doctrine or the doctrine pushers. Instead, now I choose to believe that they are broken too, suffering just as I was from the weight of slavery and orphanhood and trying to make it all make sense. But there are consequences to this kind of teaching and this kind of learning. I believe that it caused me not to love the Holy Spirit but to grow skeptical of him. Even though it wasn't directly presented to me that the Holy Spirit wasn't to be trusted, that's what was communicated to my heart. I even judged him at times. My relationship with him was far from friendship. I loved Jesus and I loved the Father but I criticized the Holy Spirit.

Later in life I came to a place where I wanted to embrace the Holy Spirit. I prayed to be baptized with the Holy Spirit just like Jesus instructed the disciples to be in Acts 1. But when I did, it seemed that nothing happened or changed, at least nothing like what happened in Acts. I have heard other people who grew up in the same teaching as I did say the same thing, "I've prayed to receive the Holy Spirit, but it seemed like nothing happened to me." I have come to believe that we struggled with the same thing. Our accusation and criticism of the Holy Spirit bred a lack of trust. We had accused him of taking advantage of people or we were skeptical that his power was real to begin with. This skepticism grew a lack of trust of his character in our hearts.

Think about it like salvation. We know that if someone doesn't trust who Jesus is and that if someone doesn't really believe that he died for them, then they can't really believe in him to the extent of receiving his salvation for their life. It is the same with the Holy Spirit. So when I prayed, I believed in him and I believed that he wanted to do good things, but I didn't *trust* him so I couldn't really receive all that he had to give me.

It wasn't that long ago that I had this revelation as it relates to some of the spiritual gifts. I was on a missions trip with a team of trusted leaders. We had just returned from an evening service where my friend was operating in her gift of prophecy with an amazing amount of grace. I hadn't really ever noticed before how fluidly she could function in that gift. I had the same gift, but my operation in it had been more staccato in flow and I wasn't very confident. Later that evening while our group was debriefing, I whispered to the Father, "Why is it that she has more confidence in her gifts than I do?" As quickly as I asked it, the answer came. "Because you judged the works of my Spirit for so long, you haven't been able to fully receive all that I am," he said. At that moment, I recalled all of the times I passed judgment not only on that gift, but on many more as well. I repented that night for judging his gifts as wrong, bad, or irrelevant, and I asked the Father to forgive me for judging him and the Holy Spirit. I asked him to fill me again (a common prayer of mine now) and told him how much I loved him and his Holy Spirit. I noticed a marked change in my confidence in what I saw and heard in the Spirit. Remember how Jeremiah spoke of our confidence being in him? I had judged both the Spirit and his gifts long enough to not have faith to receive them.

I REJECT THE ENEMY'S LIES

I think all of this controversy over the third member of the Trinity is a plan of the enemy against our sonship. Think about it. If the Holy Spirit is going to lead us to our sonship, wouldn't it make sense that Satan would lead us to believe that the Spirit is untrustworthy? Those we don't trust we don't allow near us, right? Jesus prayed, "Our Father who is in Heaven"—so that's where the Father is. And Jesus ascended to the right hand of the Father, so that's where he is. But Jesus did say that he would send us a Counselor who would be with us all the time. So in my walk with Jesus, I was pretty much ignoring the one part of the Trinity that was with me here on earth. For so long, I had counted the one part of the Trinity that was given to help me, guide me, and lead me into righteousness as obsolete. He leads me to repentance, teaches me how to forgive, how to battle the enemy, and he gives me the desire to want more of Jesus, more nearness to the Father, and even more of himself. He is so very, very good.

On top of all that goodness, the Holy Spirit is our guide to sonship. He gives us wisdom and revelation into the points in our lives where the lies of the enemy were rooted in experience and given life to grow and be received. He leads us to the roots of our slavery and our orphanhood so that we can exact forgiveness and truth where needed. And I believe that the realization of who we are in Christ becomes easier and easier for our souls when we become better and better friends with the Holy Spirit. At the Last Supper, before his crucifixion, Jesus talks to the disciples and says:

> And I will ask the Father, and he will give you another Counselor to be with you forever—the Spirit of truth. The world cannot accept him, because it neither sees him nor knows him. But you know him, for he lives with you and will be in you. I will not leave you as orphans; I will come to you [...] On that day you will realize that I am in my Father, and you are in me, and I am in you. (John 14:16-18, 20)

Do you see this? He says that it is the Holy Spirit, the Spirit of truth, that tells us who we are. The Holy Spirit speaks the truth to our hearts that we are no longer orphans, but that we are in him and he is in us and he is in the Father. Look, friends, the work of clearing the debris of orphanhood and slavery from our road is our responsibility. And the Holy Spirit is our guide for the journey.

I RECEIVE THE BAPTISM

After all of my own personal searching I had to agree that being baptized in the Holy Spirit was God's idea and not just a crazy plan cooked up by some overly emotional charismatic crowd out to make me yell in tongues and fall over. I also had to agree that we may receive a deposit of the Holy Spirit when we choose to have faith in the work of Christ on the cross and partake of John's baptism, but we can also be baptized and receive an invited outpouring of the goodness and life of the Holy Spirit. We can invite that presence over and over again.

Who is the Holy Spirit to you? Have you believed in doctrine that has created a scenario in your mind where the Holy Spirit is unimportant, obsolete or even scary? Is the Holy Spirit a friend or a stranger? A part of the Trinity you explicitly trust or the one member that you've decided you'd like to keep at a distance?

Have you judged the works of the Holy Spirit? Does the doctrine you believe teach you to rule out certain gifts as obsolete? Have you decided that certain denominations are wrong because they operate in these gifts?

Have you judged believers who rejected the Holy Spirit or his gifts? Have you isolated yourself from believers who don't embrace the Holy Spirit in the same way you do?

Do you talk to the Holy Spirit? Have you ever prayed to be baptized with the Holy Spirit? Do you want more of him? You know, all you have to do is ask.

Let's pray about some of these things. Take some time and invite the Holy Spirit to join you and examine your heart. Pray any of the following prayers that you feel apply to you.

NOW I PRAY

Father, I repent for judging the works and actions of your Holy Spirit. I also repent for judging your people who offended me with their actions and their attitudes as it related to your gifts. I recognize that they too were suffering under the effects of the garden and that their slave and orphan tendencies caused them to find a place by having a gift. Help me to forgive them for making me feel small and lacking.

I repent for judging believers who haven't received the work or the person of the Holy Spirit. I repent for judging them as not quite having it all together, and for thinking that I did! Help me to love and deal with the pride in my heart.

I repent for bringing any division in my heart from believers who believe differently than I do as it relates to the Holy Spirit. I want you to teach me how to forgive and love them in the midst of their brokenness.

Holy Spirit, I love you. I want to be baptized by you. I choose to submit my intellect to your supernatural ways. I don't understand them and I realize I won't often be able to explain them. This has made me fear you in the past, but today I repent of that fear and choose to receive the perfect love of the Father that casts out all fear.

And as all fear has left, I encourage you to pray in your prayer language. Remember, it's not supposed to make sense to your mind. Submit your mind and your need to understand to your new friend, the Holy Spirit, and trust him.

PART 3:
THE PATHWAY TO SONSHIP

GETTING READY

SONSHIP IS A JOURNEY

We all have different struggles, and I haven't shared my stories assuming that we would struggle with the exact same things. Instead, I've hoped to present the idea that sonship is a process, a journey that we all have to take. It is not a box that we can check like something on a to-do list. To think of it like this is deceiving to our hearts. Not only does it devalue the idea of our sonship, but it also indicates that the process itself should be pressed through at some intensity of speed in order to get 'er done. That only serves to appease our tendencies toward slavery.

Walking in our sonship is much like growing in marriage. I was married on November 5th, 1994, but every day of every year I fall more in love with my husband and understand more of what it means to be one with him. The name change and the ring were instant, but coming into a deeper trust, a deeper love, and the surety that it brings to my heart is a daily process and it isn't always easy. As you may know, marriage is often so hard you want to give up or decide just to coast along in neutral, not pressing in for more intimacy or understanding.

Sonship is the same. The moment we come to Jesus his blood covers us and presents us to the Father as blameless children, and we are received into his family. At that moment we are adopted by the Father. We become his sons. He pours his unconditional love out over us, and it is a never ending stream of life that we can drink from and be filled by.

However, our minds still have harmful patterns and damaging tendencies that we learned through the DNA of orphanhood and slavery. These patterns were formed when the hurtful experiences of our lives agreed with the lies of the enemy against us. These patterns, cycles and tendencies are what cover the roots of hurt in our hearts like a wax seal. The love of the Father pours over us, and as new creations we can receive so much of it. However, for those parts that are waxed by the pain of the past, his love seems just to roll off like water off a duck's back. Or, at the very best, his love is acknowledged and understood with our minds, but the wounded places in our hearts can't receive the truth that his love conveys. It is in those very parts that we need his love the most, and it is in those parts that we can't receive his love.

Getting rid of these learned patterns, cycles, and tendencies takes time and discovery; it takes divine revelation. So does removing the wax from the part of our hearts that has been affected by wounding. Pursuing healing and wholeness is a decision that must be made in full view of what it requires. It will require time, submission to a process, and openness and vulnerability to a few trusted people in your life; most of all, it will require a steadfast trust in the character of the Father. He is good. He is trustworthy. He is showering you with his love.

As we move into this the last section of the book I want to present you with something that will feel more like a workbook. Unless you take your pen and start writing your own story on the following pages, you may never realize the intended results of this book. I would also encourage you to invite a loving pastor, a caring overseer, or an influential friend into these conversations so you can have a partner to help you. Please take the time and join me as we travel further down the healing path to sonship.

Let's begin our journey together by asking the Holy Spirit to give us insight into who this special person might be for us.

PREPARING FOR THE JOURNEY

I live in the mountains of Colorado and am surrounded by hundreds of hiking opportunities. When it comes to experiencing the terrain there are two options: a) a groomed trail that is well-marked and maintained, or b) wild, uncharted territory that can be discovered one footstep at a time.

When I prepare for a hike in wild, uncharted territory I make sure I have some essentials: water, sunscreen, snacks, and my favorite guides, Chris and Tiffany. They are dear friends and awesome high country mountaineers. They are excellent at leading us to some wonderful vistas that give us a new perspective of the terrain where we live. For instance, I was surprised when I found out that a 12,000+ foot peak that I drove by frequently had knobby, bouldered hills at the top and was covered in heather. From the point of view I had normally, the peak seemed tree-covered and rocky. Not only do I get the adventure of the journey, but I get the benefit of the perspective I have when I get to the summit. If I'm going to make it to the peak to enjoy these vistas, though, I have to trust that my guides know the way, that they've read the maps, and that they see all of the pitfalls that lay on my path and they know how to maneuver around them. So with each of these adventures I always have to do the same things: prepare my mind and body, gather my essentials and connect with my guide.

Our journey to sonship is going to use these same principles. Your heart is like that wild terrain, and only the Holy Spirit knows every part of it. You need him to be your guide. If you are going to make it to the place where you gain a new perspective of yourself, then you will have to trust your guide completely. You'll have to be confident that he knows the way, can read the maps, and that he sees all the pitfalls that lay in your path and knows how to maneuver around them.

So let's approach pursuing our journey to sonship with this same strategy. First let's get prepared:

Gather your essentials: A Bible, this book, a pen, tissues, a small memo pad, and a quiet space—a place and time where you won't be interrupted for at least 20 minutes.

Prepare your mind and body: Quiet your mind from the busyness of your life. Focus your thoughts on the Father and his goodness to you. Now invite the Holy Spirit to come and join you. Let's begin by meditating on this scripture, remembering that he wants to lead you to the truth: "Search me, O God, and know my heart; test me and know my anxious thoughts. See if there is any offensive way in me, and lead me in the way everlasting" (Psalm 139:23-24).

Note: There's a good chance that you will, in this quiet space, think of something important that will tempt you away from the quiet moment you've carved out, and the enemy, no doubt, will try to drag you away from the solace into the urgency of this item and the importance of not forgetting it. So I encourage you to prepare for this with the preemptive strike known as the memo pad.

I do warfare against these distractions with a small memo pad that accompanies my workbook and Bible so that when I get distracted with a to-do, a phone call, or another need I can satisfy my mind by writing it down and not forgetting it. Later when I am ready to engage the world again, I have a list (long or short) of important things on my tiny memo pad. I take care of them and then laugh at the enemy's attempt to steal my time with the Father.

Let's involve the Holy Spirit even in these entry points to our journey. Use the space below to ask him if there is anything in your heart that is apprehensive about the journey ahead.

_____

_____

_____

_____

_____

_____

Now let's trust him to help our hearts in that place of concern and let's trust him for the time these exercises will take, the childcare they may require, and the courage that will be needed to press on. Let's pray:

"Father, help my heart to trust you in these unknown places. Help me trust you for the time and the provision at every turn to find the quiet space in my home and in my heart to deal with the deeper places that you desire to heal. I believe you want to heal my heart. You are good to me."

CONNECT WITH YOUR GUIDE

THE HOLY SPIRIT IS YOUR HEALING GUIDE

God loves you. Remember, he is pouring his love out over you in a constant flow. It is abundant, sufficient, and available for you to receive and access at all times. Look at how Paul talks about this love:

> I pray that out of his glorious riches he may strengthen you with power through his Spirit in your inner being, so that Christ may dwell in your hearts through faith. And I pray that you, being rooted and established in love, may have power, together with all the saints, to grasp how wide and long and

high and deep is the love of Christ, and to know this love that surpasses knowledge—that you may be filled to the measure of all the fullness of God. (Ephesians 3:6-19)

We are finite beings. Our lives in the natural world have a beginning and an end. But remember what Psalm 139 says? That we were formed in the depths of the earth. We were formed in the spirit realm and will continue on in the spirit realm. Isn't it funny then that we try to understand most everything with our minds? In the passage above, Paul reminds the Ephesians that it is only by the power of the Spirit that they truly grasp the width and breadth of the love of Christ. His is "the love that surpasses knowledge." Our minds can't conceive or truly understand his love for us.

I share the same heart for you as Paul had for the Ephesians—that you would know that to pursue the deepest understanding of who you are in Christ as a son is worth all the pain of visiting your brokenness again and again in order to move past the wreckage that that brokenness left in your pathway to home. And visiting that brokenness needs a chaperone. We need the Holy Spirit to lead us.

BUILDING OUR TRUST

We've embraced the Holy Spirit or at least we've chosen to be friends with him (a wonderful first step), and now we are going to ask the Holy Spirit to lead our hearts to sonship. If he's going to be our guide, it follows that we will have some questions along the way. And if we have questions, we will need answers.

The Holy Spirit is so faithful to answer us when we pursue him. Listen to this:

In the same way, the Spirit helps us in our weakness. We do not know what we ought to pray for, but the Spirit himself intercedes for us with groans that words cannot express. And he who searches our hearts knows the mind of the Spirit, because the Spirit intercedes for the saints in accordance with God's will. (Romans 8:27-28)

Isn't this a wonderful promise to grab hold of as we move into asking questions of the Holy Spirit, who is our healing guide to sonship?

LISTENING TO THE SOUND OF HIS VOICE

Let's also believe that if he's going to answer, we're going to hear him. I believe the Lord speaks to us in many different ways. Three of those ways are through the Word, through the counsel of elders, and through the Spirit. Many of us have had the Lord confirm or direct us while reading scripture and praying. And most of us have had leaders and mentors in our lives pray with us and give us some guidance.

I do find, however, that many believers struggle to have confidence in their ability to hear the voice of the Lord. The main question I hear is, "How do I know it is the Lord and not my own thoughts—or worse, the enemy trying to deceive me?" I totally understand this question and I lived much of my life with the same struggle. However, in 1998 I was part of a Bible study that gave me tools for overcoming this struggle. The study was based entirely on scripture, and it encouraged me that the Holy Spirit wanted to speak to me and that I could hear him. One of the tools I learned was to ask the Lord questions, journal what came to mind, and submit these journal entries to a trusted leader or mentor. Some call this exercise "listening prayer." This was such an effective tool for me because the journaling occupied my mind and kept me from second guessing everything. And having my husband, who is a trusted leader in my life, read my entries to see if his spirit bore witness to what I had written was helpful, as well.

Another tool I learned was to apply some basic principles that helped me discern if I was hearing the Father, myself, or the enemy. You can use these, too, in your own discernment process:

1. The enemy is called the "accuser of our brothers" in Revelation 12:10. The Holy Spirit will not accuse you or anyone else.
2. The enemy is adversarial and his work is to come against us. But Romans 8:31 tells us that the Father is for us all.
3. The enemy brings turmoil and confusion. Jesus is the Prince of Peace, and his is a peace unlike what the world offers (John 14:27).

Let's try this together. Find a quiet space and make sure you have 20 minutes to give to this exercise. I'm going to give you a question to ask the Father and I want you to use the space below to write the first things that come to your mind without judging them at all. Feel free to share what you write with a trusted mentor or spiritual leader who knows you well and who can help you discern the voices you hear.

Let's ask the Father, "How do you feel about me today?"

_____

_____

_____

_____

_____

_____

_____

_____

_____

Let's share our thankful hearts with Jesus. Write down some ways you've recognized his goodness toward you this week.

_____

_____

_____

_____

_____

_____

Let's ask the Holy Spirit, "How do you see me today?"

_____

_____

_____

_____

_____

_____

_____

QUIET THE DISSONANT VOICES

Another tool for learning how to hear the Lord is to take your thoughts captive. Look at what Paul says in 1 Corinthians 10:5: "We demolish arguments and every pretension that sets itself up against the knowledge of God, and we take captive every thought to make it obedient to Christ."

In order to "demolish arguments and every pretension," we must take our thoughts captive and submit them in obedience to Jesus. When I'm praying for myself or someone else, I submit any impressions I have from the Holy Spirit and take them captive to make them obedient to Christ. In doing so, I trust that if it is the enemy trying to distract me or lead me astray the thought will diminish in the presence of Christ. And if the thought is my own it will also have to submit to Christ because I have chosen that position in my heart. But if it is his thought, it will remain.

How do I do this? Practically speaking, I first began by visualizing the thought (in picture form) being shot into the hands of the Lord, where he takes it into his authority. I even instruct my children about how to use their minds to rule over their thoughts, take them into captivity and send them on to the Lord. Their little boy minds always have an original way to deal harshly with their thoughts or put them into some kind of space capsule and send them to the Father. Even though now I can take a thought captive just by speaking it out, I still find that there are times that I get bombarded by a unusually distracting thought. In these times I visualize an imprisonment of the thing and find that some kind of catapult still works to subdue it to its rightful place in God's hands.

Let's try it. Write down a thought that is plaguing you right now. Let's practice shooting it into the hands of the Lord so he can rule it. Whether it's fear, accusation, shame, condemnation—whatever it is—write it down in the lines that follow:

_____

_____

_____

_____

_____

_____

Let's practice this prayer aloud: "Jesus, I take this thought that I know is not from you and I make it my captive. I am no longer ruled by it. Instead I bring it to you."

Use the space below to continue taking your thoughts captive and shooting them into the hands of the Father. I bring this thought:

_____

_____

_____

And I put it in your hands. I don't know what to do with it myself, but I don't trust it. I bring it to you and place it under your authority. I ask you to rule over it so it will not rule over me. I bring this thought:

_____

_____

_____

And I put it in your hands. I don't know what to do with it myself, but I don't trust it. I bring it to you and place it under your authority. I ask you to rule over it so it will not rule over me. I bring this thought:

_____

_____

_____

And I put it in your hands. I don't know what to do with it myself, but I don't trust it. I bring it to you and place it under your authority. I ask you to rule over it so it will not rule over me.

By disciplining myself to take my thoughts captive, I've come to recognize the voice of the Lord more quickly over time. You can practice this all the time, every day. Just as awkward as it may have felt to start addressing the Father, the Son, and the Holy Spirit...all three...more often, this too may feel uncomfortable at first. I guarantee it will become natural because it is your nature in Christ to rule over lies and only believe the truth. It's just like when you make a new friend. Your new friend will call you and clarify who it is when you answer the phone. But over time spent together talking and listening, you begin to identify his or her voice and he or she doesn't have to tell you who it is when you answer anymore. This is how it is with hearing the Lord; you have to learn to discern his voice from your own voice and the deceptive voice of the enemy.

BECOMING CONFIDENT IN GOD

The definition of the word soul is varied and debatable. The definition I would like to operate with is this one: Your soul is your mind, your will and your emotions.

Remember in the last section how we told our thoughts what to do? In essence we were ruling our thoughts; we were directing them to submit to a higher, more trustworthy authority—the Father. We can do the same thing with our will and our emotions. Being someone who is self-controlled is simply being someone who controls, directs or rules his or her will by choosing to submit it to the Father. Ruling our emotions is very much the same. We choose to submit our feelings to the Father instead of letting them rule us and tell us who we are. When we rule something, we enact our God-given authority over that thing.

Our ability to rule our souls is vital to our ability to believe the truth. And our ability to believe the truth is the foundation of our sonship. If I tell you that you are a beautiful, beloved son or daughter of the Father, but you are having a bad hair day, you ate three extra donuts for breakfast, and you are struggling with wanting to gossip about a friend, do you think you'll be able or even willing to accept that truth about yourself? Probably not. Why not? Because in that moment you are letting your soul rule the truth about who you are.

If you, however, can build your skills at ruling your soul, you can live in the truth all the time.

So practically speaking, how do we rule our souls? Let's take the example I just gave. I tell you how beautiful you are in the Father as his son. You, however, are having a bad hair day, so your mind remembers that last glance in the mirror and the thought pops into your head, "Beautiful, lady? Please! Can you see this mess on my head?" But in that very moment you choose to submit that thought to the Father and rule it. You say, "Father, I submit to you the thought of my hair that prevented me from receiving the words that say that I'm beautiful."

Then you remember the three extra donuts you had at breakfast and you immediately feel fat. Your emotions sense the shame of your indulgence. Shame starts to take its toll, and you choose to submit that feeling (which, by the way, is never sent by the Father) to the Father and confess it. You say, "Father, I submit this feeling of shame to you. I overindulged at breakfast, but I know I am still received by you and am not rejected in the midst of making a poor choice."

Then, you deal with the temptation to deflect all these bad feelings you are submitting to the Father by telling me about someone else's issues. Gossip would most definitely distract you from your bad feelings, especially if the news is negative. But again, you choose to submit your will to the Father and agree with his desire to bless the person you are about to expose and not share bad information about them. Look at that! You just ruled your soul!! It's not complicated, it just takes the split second to stop and recognize what is happening in your thoughts (mind), your desire (will), and your feelings (emotions) and choose to rule it and submit it to God's authority.

Let's try it. I'm going to make a statement and then I want you to use the lines below to write down the response in your mind, your will, and your emotions. Here we go.

You are God's dream. Without you, life just wouldn't be the same for him. He cherishes you. He cherishes who you are. You are a treasure to him and he enjoys just watching you and taking in the marvel that you are to him.

The response of your mind:

_____

_____

The response of your will:

_____

_____

The response of your emotions:

_____

_____

Now, for how ever many thoughts, feelings, or desires you had that wanted to combat, argue, or dispute that truth, I want you to rule them one at a time.

Write down the words you used to submit the thoughts that opposed the truth or, if you used a picture to submit them as I have, draw that picture.

_____

_____

Journal about how you ruled a desire you had when you read my statement. For example, you might have wanted to throw the book across the room in protest. Write down how you ruled your will.

_____

_____

Jot down the way you ruled the feelings or emotions that stood in opposition to my statement of the Father's love for you.

_____

_____

Now, can your heart receive the truth of that statement a little bit better? Did you feel anything happen when you ruled your soul in that exercise? Write how you feel now below.

_____

_____

_____

_____

In order to live and rule in our sonship this challenge is set before us: Are we confident in God? Do we believe what he says about us? Do we have certainty about his goodness and his love for us? Do we trust his character? By submitting our mind, will, and emotions, we surely agree that he can help us learn the truth about who we are.

103

So now, we have a choice to make. We can allow the Holy Spirit to come into our daily lives and renew our understanding of God's love. We can rule our souls and believe the truth that he can restore our trust in a trustworthy God. Or, we can choose not to believe the truth of what God's love really means, and we can choose to keep trusting in the old voices. I believe that Jesus is the antidote to the lies of the enemy that come against the perfect character of God and that it is time for us to choose to trust him.

Remember again what Jeremiah said about trusting in your own strength or in the strength of others instead of trusting solely in the Father? He said, "But blessed is the man who trusts in the Lord, whose confidence is in him" (Jeremiah 17:7). Sometimes we can trust Jesus to save us from our sins, and that's about it. When it comes to health, or finances, or relationships, we often put our trust right back in ourselves. The words of Jeremiah are much different than that brief moment of trust. This passage defeats the idea of a compartmentalized faith and speaks of a confidence in the good and trustworthy character of God. This goes directly against the words of accusation the enemy brought to Adam and Eve in the garden. To have our confidence in the Father, in Jesus, and in the Holy Spirit is to do direct warfare against the indictments the enemy planted in our hearts toward God.

Write down five of the most important areas of your life (family, children, career pursuits, etc.).

_____

_____

_____

_____

_____

Now, for each one write out how you have felt about God's ability to love you in regards to it. Have you trusted him? Have you had confidence in him? Or have your suffered from the lies of the enemy?

_____

_____

_____

_____

_____

_____

_____

_____

_____

_____

_____

Now for each of those same areas of life, write down how you will rule your soul and trust God to be good to you in it.

_____

_____

_____

_____

_____

_____

_____

_____

_____

_____

_____

Commit this scripture to memory and choose to rule your soul until you can believe every word of it for yourself: "For the Lord is good and his love endures forever; his faithfulness continues through all generations" (Psalm 100:5).

TRAPS BENEATH THE PITFALLS

WHAT IS A "PITFALL"?

In the natural, a pitfall is well-covered or concealed trap. Spiritually speaking, it is much the same. A pitfall is any situation on our journey to sonship that has been concealing the trap of either slavery or orphanhood from us. We know now that orphanhood and slavery are where the enemy wants us to live. He wants those identities to become our reality. Therefore, understanding more about each of them and how they manifest in our lives is very important. In the next chapter we are going to do some exercises to discover where these pitfalls lie and how to identify them. But first we need to understand a little bit more about the traps that lie beneath them and how they function.

A PARABLE SHOWS THE TRAPS

Do you remember the parable Jesus told about The Two Boys Who Didn't Know How Much Daddy Loved Them? You may not recognize it by that name. Most people call it the Parable of the Prodigal Son. My husband renamed this parable at a retreat we hosted last year, and he explained it in light of the fact that both boys in the story were suffering. Though we touched on the parable earlier, let's look at it together again in more detail. I want you to see that one of them was acting out of spiritual orphanhood and the other was acting out of spiritual slavery.

Jesus continued: "There was a man who had two sons. The younger one said to his father, 'Father, give me my share of the estate.' So he divided his property between them.

"Not long after that, the younger son got together all he had, set off for a distant country and there squandered his wealth in wild living. After he had spent everything, there was a severe famine in that whole country, and he began to be in need. So he went and hired himself out to a citizen of that country, who sent him to his fields to feed pigs. He longed to fill his stomach with the pods that the pigs were eating, but no one gave him anything.

"When he came to his senses, he said, 'How many of my father's hired men have food to spare, and here I am starving to death! I will set out and go back to my father and say to him: Father, I have sinned against heaven and against you. I am no longer worthy to be called your son; make me like one of your hired men.'" So he got up and went to his father.

"But while he was still a long way off, his father saw him and was filled with compassion for him; he ran to his son, threw his arms around him and kissed him."

"The son said to him, 'Father, I have sinned against heaven and against you. I am no longer worthy to be called your son.'

"But the father said to his servants, 'Quick! Bring the best robe and put it on him. Put a ring on his finger and sandals on his feet. Bring the fattened calf and kill it. Let's have a feast and celebrate. For this son of mine was dead and is alive again; he was lost and is found.' So they began to celebrate.

"Meanwhile, the older son was in the field. When he came near the house, he heard music and dancing. So he called one of the servants and asked him what was going on. 'Your brother has come,' he replied, 'and your father has killed the fattened calf because he has him back safe and sound.'

"The older brother became angry and refused to go in. So his father went out and pleaded with him. But he answered his father, 'Look! All these years I've been slaving for you and never disobeyed your orders. Yet you never gave me even a young goat so I could celebrate with my friends. But when this son of yours who has squandered your property with prostitutes comes home, you kill the fattened calf for him!'

"'My son,' the father said, 'you are always with me, and everything I have is yours. But we had to celebrate and be glad, because this brother of yours was dead and is alive again; he was lost and is found.'" (Luke 15:11-32)

In this parable, the younger son decided life on the farm wasn't that great. So he asked for his inheritance, gathered his things and left to find "greener pastures." He did just what spiritual orphans do. He went to find his identity. We know from the story that he found parties and prostitutes and a pig sty in the end. After he's spent all his money and has finally resorted to eating pig slop he comes to his senses. He knew how he had hurt his dad by disrespecting him and squandering his inheritance of the estate on women and wild living. So how does he return? Much like I did after my wild stint in college. He and I both had an "I'll-have-to-pay-for-this" mentality. He decided that his father's servants had it way better than he did. And his expectation was that his father had disowned him, so he prepared his re-entry speech with "I am no longer worthy to be called your son; make me like one of your hired men."

Doesn't some of that sound familiar? It does to me. Let's look at what his dad did for him. He sees him from far away, which tells me that he, for however long his son had been gone, had been glancing down the road for him. Can you imagine that he had played this scene out in his mind before, in hopes that it would someday come to be? And when it does, he can hardly contain himself. I imagine he rubbed his eyes a bit to see if it was his own hopeful thoughts playing tricks on his mind, or if it was really happening. When he saw it was really his son coming home, he tore off down the road to meet him.

This was a parable Jesus was teaching, so we know this is a picture of our heavenly Father. Look closely at what he does. The son made the speech he'd practiced, but without missing a beat, almost as if he ignored that nonsense, the father called to one of his servants to bring him a robe. In that time, a family robe could only be worn by an honored son. It was a symbol of identity, prominence, and worth. He put the robe on his son. Then the father called for his servants to bring a ring for his son's finger, a pair of sandals for his feet, and a fattened calf to slaughter for a party to celebrate his return. The ring, in those days, was a symbol of authority. So without a period of testing or probation, the father gladly gave his son all the authority he had. Then he put sandals on his son's wandering feet. Can you imagine what his servants must have been muttering as they gathered these things? "Doesn't he know that boy just came back to fill his tank? He'll be gone again in no time. Sandals are the last thing I'd give this boy!" But the father wanted to show his son that he trusted him. By placing the sandals on his feet, he was saying, "Son, you are mine. You can come and go as you please!" Finally, there was the fattened calf and the party. With one last explosive gesture he wanted his son to recognize and receive the depths of his abundant love for him. He wanted his son to see that there was no one else like him and that to have him back meant everything to him.

Back at the farm, the oldest son heard a ruckus. "What's going down over there," he asked. The servant replied, "Your brother has returned from his wandering and your dad is giving him a party." That wasn't really what the older son expected to hear. He was furious, and like a spoiled brat he refused to go into the party and sat outside sulking. The Father, however, has mercy on him as well, and he went out to find him. He begged him to join in the fun, but the older son responded in classic slave form: "Look! All these years I've been slaving for you and never disobeyed your orders." Can you imagine the look on the Father's face? All this time he thought his son had stayed on the farm to be near him, only to find that he was working to win his dad's attention and favor. Then the son brought an accusation that revealed even more of his heart: "Yet you never gave me even a young goat so I could celebrate with my friends."

Here he discounted the father's love for him and only expected a goat, not a fattened calf. He also revealed where his affections were because he didn't plan to have a celebration with his Father but with his friends. He just wanted the abundance so he could party with his pals. His disdain for his brother was solid and you can see how he had judged his Father's celebratory love for his brother: "But when this son of yours who has squandered your property with prostitutes comes home, you kill the fattened calf for him!" Can you see the knowledge of good and evil at work in him? The story ends with the Father telling the older son, "My son, you are always with me…didn't you know that all I've had this whole time has been yours? I thought your brother was dead but he is alive, he was lost but now he is found and I must celebrate him!" The older son was blinded by the slavery in his heart. He couldn't see that his Father's love was always there for him, that everything that his Father owned was already his and that his Father loved just having him around, whether he was working in the fields or not.

I love that parable even more now that I can see both of those boys and their issues and the Father's loving response to both of them. I've seen myself act like each one of them in my own bondage to orphanhood and slavery. Did you recognize yourself in either of them? Have you heard your own heart respond to the Father like one or both of the sons?

We established earlier that orphanhood and slavery are both evidences of our broken nature from our old DNA. This brokenness has caused disease in our hearts. And like any other heart disease we need to identify its cause. We do this by looking at the symptoms. The symptoms of both the orphan heart and the slave heart can often be identified in cycles. The broken action renders an unhelpful response, which in turn begs for another action to hopefully gain the response necessary to satisfy the broken heart.

In order to move on into wholeness we need to get clarity into our own hearts. We don't really know our hearts that well. We need to get help from the Holy Spirit. Let's invite the Holy Spirit to guide us as we read this next section.

Remember how I said that we would need the map of our memories to lead us to the roots of our orphanhood and slavery? Well, in order to gain clear understanding we are going to have to learn how to read the map. Of course, our guide, the Holy Spirit, is going to be there with us to explain the topography and give us the keys. But there are some basic cycles we can look for in ourselves that will give us a hint as to which traps we are suffering from.

THE TRAP OF THE ORPHAN CYCLE

This is a quick overview of some ways in which the orphan spirit can conduct itself in cycles or patterns:

> I behave in search of identity – I do things I regret – I feel bad – I hope that someone will accept me – I look for love in all the wrong places – I feel bad about myself – I hope that someone will take me in and love me – I try to prove myself by becoming awesome – I fail at some point – I feel bad – I hope that someone will forget my failure and take me in and love me – and so on and so on

Do you see any of your own behavior in the above cycle? Use these lines to write what the Holy Spirit is revealing to you about your own orphan cycle.

_____

_____

_____

_____

_____

_____

A quick look at cycles helps us get a bird's eye view on how the orphan heart desires to meet its own need for healing. Next, let's look deeper into the pathology of the orphan heart.

Looking for Identity

The heart of the orphan is looking for identity. Therefore, it will often act out in search of someone who will name it, recognize it, give it purpose. In the natural, as children grow up they often try different sports, activities, and even fashions to see what seems to fit who they are. This is actually quite normal and healthy. The heart of the spiritual orphan does this as well, but not in a healthy way. Instead of experimenting in order to understand what its gifts are or what its style is, the heart of the orphan looks to its peers to identify it, to tell it who it is.

Only God was meant to give us our identity. Therefore, anytime we try to find it in other people we extract from them more than they can give. We are like a bottomless well of need in that relationship. Then our orphan heart feels wounded and wonders why that relationship let us down and didn't _love_ us enough. For those who love someone who has an orphan heart the question is often, "What have I done this time?" And the one suffering from the trap of orphanhood feels let down by those he or she is extracting his or her identity from. This happens because there is no way to fill the tank of the heart of the orphan. Only the Father can tell the orphan who he or she really is, so neither person in this relationship is satisfied.

For example, Cindy loves to care for people. She has a wonderful hospitality gift yet struggles to find ways to let it really flow. This isn't because there aren't people to host or care for. It is simply because Cindy suffers from an orphan heart. Her need to be identified and recognized leaves her heart always in lack. That pathology in her heart has created a need for affirmation of a specific kind. Because this need is so great and so particular, it is hard for Cindy's love well to be filled. Cindy has a reason in almost every relationship as to why that person has failed her. Her friends and family pour and pour love into Cindy's love well, but so much of it leaks out that she continually feels like she's running on empty. She feels happy for a bit after receiving words of love, but in a short amount of time she falls prey to the enemies lies about her and believes most everything he says about how people have let her down... again. She struggles constantly with the fear of being rejected. Not only can Cindy not receive the love that people have for her at the deepest, most necessary parts of her heart, but she also is prevented from expressing her gifts of care and hospitality for others because her orphan heart drives them away.

Needing Love and Protection

The heart of the orphan is also in need of love, affirmation, and protection. Children desiring these act out in both positive and negative ways to test the love of their parents.

Again, the Father's love is more than enough for us, but when it cannot be received, there is a deficit in that wounded and waxed part of our hearts. Like we saw in Cindy's case, this deficit often draws more from a relationship than is appropriate. Crossing boundaries, setting inappropriate expectations, and demanding more allegiance than is right for the level of relationship are all evidences that the heart of the orphan is at work. In these cases, someone must pay up or be hurt.

Thomas, for example, is a great guy. Highly intelligent, the life of the party, and über responsible. But he is deeply in need of the Father's love, and the pain of his childhood has waxed the part of his heart that can truly receive affirmation, love and protection. When he was ten years old, he was put in a situation where he not only had to provide for himself, but also watch after his younger sister. The DNA of orphanhood agreed with what those experiences spoke to his little ten year old heart: "No one is looking out for you; you will always have to take care of yourself." Now as an adult he puts unreal expectations on his relationships, testing them to see if they can measure up to what he needed as a child. His demand for communication at a certain level and for a high level of commitment as well, combined with a fear of rejection create room for disappointment for almost every relationship. He, too, has a bottomless love well, and no matter how much a person pours in, within a short amount of time that person will find that he or she has failed Thomas again.

Desiring a Place of Importance

The heart of the orphan always needs to prove itself. It needs to prove it can be something one day despite its plight in life. In fact, as the heart of the orphan "grows up," it can often look like the self-made man. There is pride associated with accomplishments. There is a great need for others to see how well the orphan has done and applaud him or her. Often an orphan enters a room, name drops, immediately hands out a business card, or tells unending stories of his or her awesome adventures. The orphan is about him or herself; the orphan isn't sure of his or her place in the world yet, and so most of his or her life's work is about carving a place out. This part of the orphan heart is also seen in the person who puts his or her identity in work or career pursuits. This person is often interested in being introduced as that thing he or she does.

Remember the story about how I needed people to know what I did in order for them to know who I was? How I orchestrated conversations in order to make room for my "rock star" status to have a place to land? And how if that wasn't dazzling enough for them I would create opportunities to tell about who I knew in order to impress? It was not just pathetic, it was tiring. I was trying so hard to be *somebody*.

Let's Examine

Holy Spirit, please reveal to me the specific ways my heart suffers from orphanhood. Write what he reveals to you.

_____

_____

_____

_____

Let's Repent

Father, I repent of acting like an orphan. I know that is not who I am, but I often wonder who I am to you. I wonder if you'll protect me, take care of me, and love me. Please help me identify the places in my life where the seeds of orphanhood have been allowed to grow. Show me the experiences, offenses, and hurts that have been the fertile soil in which the lies of orphanhood have a place to thrive. Help me to forgive each one.

On these lines, express your heart to the Father; tell him in what ways you desire to turn away from your instincts toward orphanhood.

_____

_____

_____

_____

THE TRAP OF THE SLAVE CYCLE

This is a quick overview of some ways in which the slave spirit can conduct itself in cycles or patterns:

> I work to prove I am worthy – I fail to prove it – I feel bad – I hope that the master (or those in charge) will forgive me and take me back – I try to work for a better position – I hurt someone else in the process – I feel bad – I hope that the person I hurt and the master will forgive me and take me back – I try my best to do everything perfectly – I fail to care for the people I love because I am working so hard to do everything perfectly - I fail at being perfect – I feel bad, both for failing and for hurting the ones I love – I hope the master and the loved ones forgive me and take me back – I compare myself to others in the midst of feeling bad so I can feel that I've achieved something – I find someone who has achieved more – I feel bad about myself again – and so on and so on.

Do you recognize this pattern in your own behavior? Use the space below to write what the Holy Spirit is revealing to you about your own slave cycle.

_____

_____

_____

_____

_____

Working for Worth, Love, and Acceptance

The heart of the slave must work to earn love, acceptance and favor. The slave's nearness to the master, the person in charge, or other slaves is determined by how well he or she has performed. If the slave follows all the rules and does the work that is required, he or she will earn a level of acceptance that other slaves don't have. In having a better position than others, slaves believe they also have more love than others and therefore have more favor, respect, honor, love, acceptance, etc. Better positioning to the slave also equates with "nearness." That's why nearness means more work for the slave heart. But if slaves break a rule or don't follow through with instructions, then they can lose their position and thus have less favor, respect, honor, love, acceptance, etc. This change in position separates them from those they seek to please until they can learn to behave better, serve more diligently, and earn a better place. This is why, to slaves, the kingdom is about achieved levels of love, acceptance, and favor from both God and man. So instead of looking like a journey with a father, the slave's journey looks more like a ladder or a mountain where the higher he or she climbs, the nearer he or she is to the master. It is sad, but it is a true feeling among many believers when they are being introduced to the idea of sonship. Through the lens of a slave, becoming a son just looks like more work to do.

Take Stacy, for example. Stacy loves people. She loves to serve people, but she finds herself overextended quite often by saying yes to too many people and too many commitments. She finds that when she is helping, volunteering, and working for others that she feels fulfilled and all seems right in the world. She would never admit that she was working for someone else's approval or acceptance, but when all of her self-sacrifice and helpfulness doesn't render the results she hoped for, she finds herself depressed and feeling rejected. She has a hard time taking a day off and even finds herself judging people who don't work as much as she does as lazy. She struggles to enjoy her life and easily falls into depression. She can't see how valuable she is unless she is performing and performing well. Failure is not an option.

The End Justifies the Means

The heart of the slave can justify many casualties on its way to be near the master or in any place of honor. The slave's trek up the mountain (since it is not a journey) may require stepping on the heads of other slaves in order to attain the elevated position they desire. And because this elevated position puts him or her nearer to the master, he or she can justify using, abusing, and hurting other slaves in order to advance his or her position. In the world's system we recognize this as dirty business, or dirty politics. But often in Christian life, if someone gets hurt because a slave achieves something "for God," then that person was not in the Lord's will or didn't have his or her heart right to begin with. We all know people who've been hurt in the church by leaders—big and small —who put their own need to be recognized, applauded, or rewarded above the needs of others. This is what slaves do.

John is a team leader for a missions organization, and he has a heart to accomplish great things for God on the field. Unfortunately, since his sights are set toward working for God instead of working with God, he runs a great risk of overlooking his team members, who need extra care and attention. In his mind, his team members are there to do work, and if their personal problems get in the way, they should just go home! John's slave heart makes excuses for why team members get hurt and for why their hurts have nothing to do with him and the goals he sets for the team. The team begins to fall apart one by one; yet to John, each is just dealing with his or her own sin issues and needs just to get over it!

Comparison is a Must

The heart of the slave must also compare itself to other slaves in order to make sure that it is right, and thus be received and seen by the master. When the intent of the heart is to be right in order to be accepted, it can not only affect the slave and those he uses, but it can also affect those he leads. Have you ever wondered what causes church splits? It is the heart of the slave. When "they are wrong and we are right," then we must separate ourselves. Healthy family doesn't divorce itself because of differing opinions or views, it just learns to love past the misunderstanding and sees the best. But when the heart of a slave enters into kingdom family life then right thinking trumps relationship, especially if it secures a nearer position to the Father. The right position validates the separation.

Karl is a banker, a believer, and a Bible study leader at his fellowship. Doctrine is very important to Karl. He's been known to pick fights over the interpretation of scripture and doesn't have any friends who don't agree with his point of view. He struggles in most every part of his life to make sure he is doing that thing right. He also struggles with the need to be perfect in most everything. He feels extra good when he can compare his way of doing something to someone else's way and prove to himself again that that person is wrong and he is right. Karl spends most of his time improving, doing it better. In his home, his marriage, his parenting, his work, his Christianity. His hard work is applauded in his church congregation and Karl is recognized as having it all together. What his congregation doesn't see is that Karl's need for perfection presses a weight onto his wife and kids for perfection, as well. His wife and children struggle constantly to meet up to his level of "good enough." And Karl, too, constantly struggles with feeling bad about himself and feels even worse when he finds someone else who is "doing it better" than he does.

Let's Examine

Holy Spirit reveal to me the specific ways my heart suffers from slavery. Write what he reveals to you.

_____

_____

_____

_____

Let's Repent

Father, I repent of acting like a slave. I know that is not who I am, but I struggle to combat the feelings that tell me you will love me less if I don't do things right. Please help me identify the places in my life where the seeds of slavery have been allowed to grow. Show me the experiences, offenses, and hurts that have been fertile soil in which the lies of slavery have a place to thrive. Help me to forgive each one.

On these lines, express your heart to the Father; tell him in what ways you desire to turn away from your instincts toward slavery.

_____

_____

_____

_____

_____

_____

IDENTIFY THE PITFALLS

RESPONDING TO PITFALLS

We are really well-equipped for the journey ahead now. We've prepared our minds and bodies, gathered our supplies, connected to our Holy Spirit guide and examined the traps that the pitfalls lead to. We've learned what the traps are all about and why it is so important to be able to understand how they operate. Now we must learn to identify the pitfalls.

Last year I ran a half marathon in Leadville, CO, the highest incorporated city in the country at 10,152 feet above sea level. The race traced the edges of Turquoise Lake, and the race website stated that this was a trail run with 1/3 of the trail paved. As a novice runner I assimilated the word trail into my previous race experience, which was to run on a dirt path that wound its way through Colorado Springs. Plus, I'm a city girl and a trail in my book is usually a paved pathway that runs between trees planted by the Parks Department. I had trained for the added 2,000 feet of elevation change from my hometown, but I wasn't quite ready for the different definition of trail.

The race started on an uphill road that served as the entrance to the campgrounds around the lake...so far so good. My husband and two boys met me at the end of the paved road with high fives and some Gatorade as the trail portion of the race began. What I encountered for the next nine miles was pretty much your standard, barely worn hiking trail on the side of a mountain! There I was, in the race, and I couldn't stop. So I continued to press through, thinking that at the next turn the trail would flatten, widen, and smooth itself out. It did not. Instead, the next eight miles became even more treacherous, with pitfalls at every turn. Sometimes there were tree trunks fallen on the trail; sometimes rain had washed out a section of the trail, leaving a dangerous hole. There were boulders to climb, streams to cross, and even a sandy beach to run through just before the end of the race. I didn't win...no, no... way far away from 1st place. But I finished.

Thinking back to that race, I notice now what my body did when it thought it was going to be injured by the many pitfalls I encountered as I ran. It automatically ignited impulses that tried to compensate for what had just happened to it. Several times my foot got caught on one of the many huge roots that twisted themselves over the path and almost made me bite it. But most of the time I didn't even know I had tripped until my body started trying to regain its balance, my arms flying out in front of me and my heart racing with the sudden burst of adrenaline. Each time my body was put in a potentially hazardous situation, it compulsively fired a message clicking my parts into gear that would help me keep my balance and not fall flat on my face. Every time I encountered one of these hazards that purposed to trip me up, my body automatically tried to protect itself and keep me safe.

This is exactly what happens in our souls when we encounter a pitfall on our journey to sonship. Some kind of automatic, compulsive response is ignited in us that tries to right the situation and protect us. The response may be physical, mental, or emotional and in every case it is serving to protect. Protect ourselves from what? you might ask. Protection from the lie that is waiting at the bottom of the pitfall. The lie that is trying to define us and identify who we are and who the Father is to us—the trap of the orphan and the slave.

The ignited response can also be seen as compulsive self-preservation or involuntary self-defense. It tries to protect us and defend us against the lies of orphanhood and slavery and against what they say about who we are or who we are not. I believe these pitfalls in our spiritual journeys are the places where a single word, event, or gesture from another person or circumstance sends us into automatic reactions. And because these automatic reactions seem like safety to us, we don't realize that they are the evidence of a problem...one that we should and can rule over. However, if we're paying attention, it is possible to identify the pitfall, notice the compulsive response, and learn how to bring the authority of Jesus over all of it.

In this chapter we're going to learn how to do just that. We'll look at these compulsive and automatic responses as clues that we've encountered a pitfall. We'll then use these clues and other information from our memories to help us identify the flint that, when struck by a hard situation, ignites the response. And finally, we'll identify the trap that lies beneath the pitfall...the lies of the enemy and the false identity that he is trying to keep us ensnared in.

We will allow our Holy Spirit guide to speak to us, and we will trust that we hear him. Remember, he was sent by Jesus with the promise to lead us to our sonship. It is his delight to uncover the pitfalls of the enemy and the traps of orphanhood and slavery. Let's move forward on our journey and trust our Spirit guide completely.

Here's some good news to get us started: In Jesus, we already have the victory over these traps. Let's take hold of it!

LOOKING FOR THE PITFALL

The Hurtful Situation

The way we can detect a pitfall is by identifying a hurtful event, conversation, or situation that ignited a response that seemed automatic or almost involuntary.

Let me give you an example of a pitfall by telling you about one of mine.

I was working on my computer at a cafe when my friend Sheila, who had come to town, texted me about getting together with her and some mutual friends, Amy and Nick. I don't have a close relationship with Amy and Nick, but I admire them and am always honored to be invited to their home. I texted back that this was a great plan and asked, "What time?" Sheila texted that she'd get in touch with Amy about times and get back to me soon. About 20 minutes later I received a text from Amy that said, "I just want to keep it family this time...Sheila didn't know that...catch you next time."

Immediately, I clicked back to the text from Sheila and my responses to her to see if I had said anything that was offensive. Maybe I had misunderstood Sheila's text to begin with. My body warmed up with embarrassment. Maybe I thought I was invited when I wasn't. I was hurt that I was rejected. For the next 30 minutes I compulsively kept grabbing my cell phone to read and re-read my texts to try to figure out what went wrong. Amy, who was a very sweet woman, texted later with an invitation to get together the next week for lunch. I immediately fired back a text that said, "I'm in a busy season and won't be able to break away for a while...tonight was my only opening."

I know that situation wasn't meant to inflict pain. But my response to defend myself was almost involuntary, and my compulsive actions tipped my heart off to the fact that I had hit something deeper than a little misunderstanding from a friend.

Now it's your turn. Ask the Holy Spirit to take you to a memory of a hurtful situation, conversation, or encounter that he wants to deal with. Write down all of the details you can remember from this encounter.

The Compulsive Response

Now look at the details of the situation. Can you easily identify a response that seemed almost automatic? Ask the Holy Spirit to point out your compulsive efforts or thoughts toward self-preservation. These thoughts, feelings or actions ignited an automatic response that served to bring balance back to your own soul or to defend yourself to the situation and the message it conveyed.

We'll use my encounter, for example: *I automatically re-read my text messages, checking for a misunderstanding or an unintended offense on my part.* My compulsive action of reading the texts over and over served to reinforce my thinking that I was, indeed, invited. I had to defend myself against the thought that maybe I had just misunderstood the request and had invited myself. How embarrassing that would have been. Then, I continued to compulsively check the texts to see if I had replied with anything that could have been interpreted as offensive. This again was self-preservation. I had to reinforce to myself that I was okay, and that this was not my fault.

You may not immediately recognize the involuntary response in the memory you wrote down earlier. That's okay because we're going to rely on the Holy Spirit to show us what we need to see. I'll ask some questions to get you started.

Can you remember having a desire to defend yourself in that situation? Did you go through an automatic cycle of thoughts or feelings? Were there compulsive plans to retaliate, payback, or prove something to that person? Or, like me, did you have any compulsive reactions to the situation? Write down your compulsive response. It may have been physical, emotional, or mental.

_____

_____

_____

Now ask the Holy Spirit to help you understand what you were defending and/or preserving with those compulsive actions.

_____

_____

_____

_____

_____

_____

The Wound

A flint is used to ignite a fire. The flint strikes steel, creating a spark that ignites tender. In the spirit realm this same process happens when a difficult situation strikes against a wound in our hearts—it ignites a response. The wound is a feeling, thought, or opinion of ourselves that already exists in us. When it collides with a hurtful situation, the collision sparks or ignites a compulsive response because it seems to reinforce the wound, or negative thought, for us again.

Let's take this into our exercise so far. The circumstance or situation you wrote down struck something that you already struggled with in your heart. Perhaps an opinion about yourself that was already resident, or something that you've already had reason to believe about yourself. That impact ignited a compulsive response in your mind or emotions as a way of defending itself against the negative opinion that the situation was reinforcing about you. The compulsive actions, thoughts, or feelings subconsciously tried to protect you from an opinion you already held of yourself.

You need the Holy Spirit to show you the wounds—the negative opinions, beliefs or feelings you have about yourself—that struck the situation or circumstance you wrote about above. The basic question will be, "How did this situation make me feel?"

Let's first examine what happened in my situation and what opinion that situation might have been reinforcing. Let's find the wound.

In my situation an invitation was retracted. I was essentially invited and then uninvited to a gathering of friends, so I felt rejected. As we saw earlier in the book, rejection is something that I already suffered from, an opinion I had about myself previously. So the situation reinforced that rejection, and I acted out in order to protect myself from that reinforced message.

Examine your situation again. Write down what happened in brief again, this time asking the Holy Spirit to bring light to your memory and show you what your wound is.

_____

_____

_____

_____

The Trap

The enemy's desire is that we will see ourselves from his perspective. His desire is that through the repetition of these negative opinions of ourselves through different difficult situations, we'll believe them as truth. When we feel like these negative opinions are reinforced around every corner, we can easily become convinced that we are who they say we are. We begin to form "I am" statements. In other words, when I feel rejected, the enemy wants me to believe that at my foundation "I am rejected." When couched in those terms, those statements become statements of being...truths about who we are.

When we hear these "I am" statements tick through our thoughts enough times, we begin to believe them. Sometimes we even say them out loud, out of our own mouths. This is precisely what the enemy is hoping for: a confession. After making a mistake, have you ever heard yourself say, "I am so stupid"? Matthew 15:18 reminds us, "the things that come out of the mouth come from the heart." Have you ever thought that what you confess with your mouth might be agreeing with what the enemy says about who you are? And if you're agreeing with him, you are disagreeing with the Father.

Let's incorporate this into our exercise. Ask the Holy Spirit to come and bring his light into your heart to show you if you've let this wound and the negative opinion about yourself that accompanies it become a confession. Write your conclusion and the "I am" statement below.

_____

_____

_____

If you've believed "I am" statements, you have probably lived into them as if they are truth. When that happens, you are trapped. Remember the pitfall is only there to cover up the trap of orphanhood or slavery. We need to recognize which trap the enemy lures us into and speak the truth to it as well.

In my situation, in which I suffered from the lie "I am rejected," I was easily lured into the trap of orphanhood. Believing I wasn't wanted or invited agreed with my wound. And once I was trapped it was easy to accuse the Father of not seeing me, not wanting me, or not protecting me. Those accusations only made sense from the position I was in. I had to renounce every one of those agreements I made against the Father.

Now it's your turn. Ask the Holy Spirit to reveal what trap the enemy was trying to ensnare you in with this wound. Was it orphanhood or slavery or some mixture of the two?

_____

_____

Ask the Holy Spirit to reveal all of the lies the enemy trapped you into believing about the Father and his character. Write them below.

_____

_____

_____

Now, let's make some confessions that will begin to work against the enemy's plans for you. Ask the Holy Spirit to speak his truth into the wound you've suffered from. What does he say about you? Write it below.

_____

_____

_____

_____

Now take what the Holy Spirit said to you about yourself and write it into a new "I am" statement of truth.

_____

_____

The Father is so good and wants to rescue us from the traps we've fallen into. Ask the Holy Spirit to speak to you about who you are. The truth. You can begin by writing the "I am" statement he gave you earlier, but ask him to tell you more.

_____

_____

_____

_____

_____

Ask the Holy Spirit to tell you who the Father is to you.

_____

_____

_____

This is a good time for you to repent of the agreements you made with the enemy about yourself and about the Father and renounce them.

I have written a prayer for you, but ask the Holy Spirit to guide you through your prayer and give you new insight and words to pray to fully release yourself from the contract you made with the enemy about your identity. This is a wonderful time to practice your prayer language as well and let the Holy Spirit minister to the deepest places that are past your natural mind.

Prayer of Repentance

Father, I recognize that I have not seen myself the way that you do. I have let the situations of my life tell me who I am. I've believed these messages so much that I've even enabled this belief to become my truth and my reality by admitting that I am (write your false "I am" statement)

_____

_____

I repent of confessing that about myself. I know that it was sin because it was in opposition of what you say is true about me. It was also sin because in that place in my heart I haven't received your love. I renounce my agreement with the enemy that I am (write the trap you have fallen into—orphan, slave, or both)

_____

_____

And I repent of believing that you are (write the lies about the Father you have agreed with)

_____

_____

So, now, I speak out the truth of who you say that I am (write your "I am" statement of truth)

_____

_____

Because I am free of those lies I can now say that you, Father, really are (write who the Father told you he was)

_____

_____

I need the Holy Spirit to help me remember who I am. I choose to speak this truth to myself over and over even if I don't feel like it is true...it really is true! *I am your favorite son! I am your favorite daughter!*

Vows of Protection

The last thing we need to address to make sure that we are no longer agreeing with the enemy's lies about who we are is the making of vows. Anytime we suffer a deep wound it is only natural to try to protect our heart for next time. This seems very rational except for the fact that in order to protect our hearts and make a vow, we have to agree with the enemy and who he says we are. We also have to agree with what he says about the Father. The vow itself is a seal of approval on the enemy's work in that part of our lives. whether we mean it to be or not. A vow can sound as innocent as "I'm not going to let anyone get that close to me again," or it can sound more like "I'll show them."

The problem is that our words have power, and the vows we make bring about whatever they say they will. Take for instance, the girl who is sexually abused in a dating relationship and vows not to let anyone get that close to her again. Well, even when her heart heals from the pain of that relationship, she will suffer from the power of her vow. Say that after her heart heals she meets the man of her dreams and falls in love. Soon after they are married she finds out that she can't enjoy intimacy. Because of the wall she put up with her vow, she's prevented herself from truly receiving her husband. He feels rejected and they find that they can't connect as they both dreamed they would, which in time begins to affect every other part of their life together.

A vow is usually made to defend the wounds, opinions, or beliefs we talked about earlier, which makes it relatively easy to detect. But sometimes a vow can be subtle. We'll use my example again to see how simple a vow can be.

My wound was rejection, but my vow wasn't "I will always be accepted," although it could have been something close to that. My vow could easily have been, "I'll work to be a person that people always want at their parties." No, my vow was more subtle. Do you remember what happened when Amy contacted me to see if I wanted to join her for lunch the next week? She was reaching out to tell me she wanted to spend time with me. How did I respond? I said, "I'm in a busy season and won't be able to break away for a while...tonight was my only opening." That was a lie. I could have made time for Amy, and at any other time I would have. But instead I made a teensy tiny vow: "I'll show her how it feels to be rejected." And I gave it right back to her. Terrible. I had to repent of making that vow and trying to hurt her heart as she had hurt mine.

Now it's your turn. Ask the Holy Spirit to help you see the vow you made in your heart when you received hurt. Don't assume you didn't make one; it could be subtle like mine. Write what he shows you below.

_____

_____

_____

_____

_____

_____

_____

Ask the Holy Spirit to show you the thought process that led you to make that vow.

_____

_____

_____

_____

_____

_____

_____

_____

_____

Now. renounce the vow you made and break the power it has had over your life. I've written a guided prayer below, but as before, ask the Holy Spirit to lead you and show you anything else you may have missed.

Prayer of Renunciation

Father, I break the vow I made (write out the vow)

_____

_____

Now, I apply Jesus' blood to the vow and I renounce the vow completely in the name of Jesus. I refuse to agree any longer with the thoughts that caused me to make that vow. I don't need to vow anything any longer because Jesus has come to show me his love—your love for me. You receive me completely as I am, and I don't need to believe anything other than what you say about me.

We have done some really great work here. Let's keep it up! In the next chapter we're going to find a few more tools that can give us even more victory over the enemy and the plans he has set against us.

THE BETTER PATH
OF FORGIVENESS

THE WORK OF FORGIVENESS

We've trekked along pretty well on the journey so far. We've identified a situation on our journey that proved to be a pitfall. We've recognized the compulsive behavior that ignited when the situation collided with our wound. We identified the wound and the "I am" statement that the enemy sought to get us to believe about ourselves. And finally we saw the trap that lay beneath the pitfall—the real life situation—that the enemy tried to ensnare us with. We've repented of believing and agreeing with the enemy's lies and we've made confessions of the truth of who we are in the Father. We could stop here and feel pretty good, but did you know the enemy could still take advantage of us in that place in our hearts? One thing that we didn't cover yet was that there were people in the midst of all of these situations. One of the ways the enemy seeks to keep us ensnared is through unforgiveness.

Unforgiveness is another way that we agree with the enemy. He doesn't want anyone to be forgiven, so when we are hurt by someone through a specific situation his desire is that we leave that situation without forgiving that person. Sometimes he tempts us by trying to convince us that that person is unforgivable. Sometimes he has us just forgive the person in a blanket "Oh, they didn't mean it" kind of way. And sometimes he lies to us and tells us we shouldn't have been offended in the first place. Well, maybe you shouldn't have been(remember the enemy traffics in partial truths), but if you were then he's luring you to leave the situation in the past without acknowledging the pain that was really there and with leaving the person and the offense unforgiven. He is sneaky. We are going to revisit the previous circumstances and apply the work of forgiveness to them, but first let's take a deeper look into the work of forgiveness.

Forgiveness is a decision. It is not an emotion or a thought, but a choice of your will. Forgiveness is a job, and the work it accomplishes is powerful and eternal. We've been commissioned in 2 Corinthians to the ministry of reconciliation—the ministry of bringing back together. This ministry is the life blood of kingdom living. In John 13:34 Jesus gave his disciples a command that has been passed on to all who find their home in the Father and their salvation in Christ: "Love one another as I have loved you."

Therefore forgiveness for us as sons is never optional. There is no grace period for unforgiveness and at no point do we get to decide that because of the severity of an offense someone deserves to wait to be forgiven. As a matter of fact, when you become a reconciler, you have more and more grace for others. You are more apt to see the wounding in their lives that led them to offend. This perspective is important because it is the Father's perspective, but we can only see from that perspective when we love as he loves and when we live in our place as sons. Unforgiveness has the power to bind us, and forgiveness has the power to set us free. Forgiveness can put to death all forms of evil, and unforgiveness can unleash evil for generations. Unforgiveness left to fester turns to bitterness. Bitterness, envy, jealousy…these are birthed out of unforgiveness. James 3:16 says that where these are allowed "there is disorder and every evil practice." When we realize the power that we hold as reconcilers, I think we will be amazed at how we can bring the winds of change not only to our relationships, but to our families, our friends, and communities as well. In order to operate in this ministry of reconciliation we need to understand the facts and dispel the myths that surround unforgiveness.

FACTS ABOUT UNFORGIVENESS

Fact #1
Unforgiveness gives the enemy legal rights to torment and imprison me.

This is true. In Matthew 18:23-35 Jesus tells the Parable of the Unmerciful Servant. I encourage you to read the whole thing, but I'll summarize the impact of the story. Jesus says that the servant who wouldn't forgive the one who owed him would be put in prison and turned over to the tormenters. Don't forget that the wicked servant himself had just been forgiven an amount by his master that was ten thousand times more than the amount he was owed. Imprisonment and legal invitation to be tormented—that's what we reap when we choose to hold an offense because someone owes us something. I'll say it again: sow in unforgiveness, and reap bondage, torture and grant the enemy legal access to your life.

Forgiving someone from your heart means that you say to that person, "You don't owe me anymore." Here's a tip for the future when you want to know if you have unforgiveness in your heart toward someone. Ask yourself, "what do they owe me?" or "is there someone who owes me something?" The answer is a good indicator of where your heart is.

Fact #2
Forgiveness must be applied to the person and the offense.

This is true. Forgiveness must be applied to the person who brought the offense, and it must be applied to the offense as well. If we only forgive one and not the other we allow for unforgiveness to fester and turn to bitterness. Although it is better not to receive an offense to begin with, it is important to be honest when we have received one and not deceive ourselves. An unrecognized offense is still unforgiveness. It is really a hurt in our heart and if we don't identify it as such and offer forgiveness, we will still be susceptible to the bondage and torment that comes with unforgiveness.

Fact #3
Forgiveness requires me to bless.

This is true. The litmus test and final work of forgiveness is whether or not you can bless the person who offended you. The desire of the Father's heart is that you be blessed, but you can't be blessed until your heart can fully release the one who owes you from the prison of unforgiveness into the freedom of blessing.

MYTHS ABOUT UNFORGIVENESS

Myth #1
To forgive means you don't feel the pain or hurt in your heart anymore.

This is not true. Forgiveness is first a choice and second a promise of healing. To forgive doesn't discount the pain you feel or immediately take it away. Nor does it mean you should wait until the anger or hurt is gone to forgive. Without forgiveness it is nearly impossible for the pain to completely go away. It is the work of forgiveness that allows for the complete healing of our souls.

Myth #2
To forgive means that I have to repair the relationship and be friends with the person that hurt me.

This is not true. Forgiveness and reconciliation go together. Forgiveness and restoration don't necessarily have to go together. Reconciliation is the work of forgiving the offender and blessing and releasing him or her from the bondage of unforgiveness. Restoration, on the other hand, is the reestablishment of relationship. If you were violated by someone and have recognized that that person is not to be trusted with your heart, then you can forgive them but you are not required to reinstate the relationship. In fact, doing so may give way for you to be violated again. This is another place where you need the Holy Spirit to lead you.

Myth #3
Forgiving the offense and forgiving the offender are one in the same.

This is not true. One person may have offended you multiple times. You may have forgiven that person, but if you heat up with anger and resentment when you are reminded of what they did to you, you need to forgive the offense as well as the offender. Close relationships like marriage often suffer from this kind of unforgiveness. The offense itself holds power over you when you choose to not forgive or when you choose to dismiss the offense and not acknowledge the pain that it caused you. This also happens mostly in close, trusted relationships. We often don't want to indict someone we respect like a parent or grandparent, or a pastor or leader who has done many good things for us. When these people hurt us we often dismiss the pain by saying, "Oh they didn't mean to hurt me." This may be true, but to discount it leaves your heart open to holding unforgiveness for the hurt that was actually there and left unacknowledged.

Now that we've gained more understanding into the work of forgiveness let's revisit our circumstances and apply what we've learned. We'll begin by writing a brief synopsis of the situation we've been working with. As in the previous chapter, we'll use my circumstance as an example.

The Situation

Let's briefly revisit the situation that we were working from in the last chapter. I was contacted by one friend inviting me to a mutual friend's house for an evening get-together. The invitation was later retracted by the hostess due to a miscommunication. Write a short synopsis of what happened in your situation below.

_____

_____

_____

_____

The Wound

Now let's think about the wound, the negative opinion, that the situation reinforced. For me, the wound was rejection and it's as if my situation was echoing the thoughts I had believed for years about myself.

Think about your wound. Was your situation reinforcing this opinion about you, as if it was trying to prove it to you? What was it saying?

_____

_____

_____

_____

The Offense

The offense is not the whole situation, but the piece of it that hurt your heart. It is important to single it out because it will need to be forgiven. The part of my situation that was hurtful was being invited and then uninvited by the hostess to a night of fun with friends.

Write down the hurtful point of the situation. Ask the Holy Spirit to reveal any subtleties that you may not see in the situation that will help the offense become clear. What do you hear?

_____

_____

_____

_____

The Offender

This is the person who was really behind the hurtful part of the situation. In my case, it was Sheila that invited me, but it was Amy who contacted me to say she had to retract the invitation. It was Amy that made me feel rejected.

Think about your situation. Who is the person behind the hurt? Ask the Holy Spirit to reveal if there is more than one. Write their names below:

_____

_____

_____

Now let's do the work of forgiving. I've written a prayer as a model, but, as always, you can feel free to pray whatever comes to your heart. Ask the Holy Spirit to lead your mind to any places where there is unforgiveness for the persons involved or for the offense and offer up forgiveness as he brings revelation.

Prayer of Forgiveness

Father, I am your son/daughter and I want to love others as you have loved me. I choose to forgive (name the offenders):

_____

_____

_____

I forgive them for the offense of (name the offense):

_____

_____

They don't owe me anymore for the hurt that they caused me. I do not hold them responsible for the wound (name the wound):

_____

_____

I suffered this wounding, whether intentional or unintentional, from them, but now I release them to be blessed by your hand. I ask that you stop the reaping of the unforgiveness I've partnered with and remove me from the bondage and torment I've placed myself under by participating in unforgiveness. Thank you for the gift of Jesus and his blood that covers me. I receive that covering and place it between me and the offense.

The Father's Perspective

Asking the Father to reveal his perspective on the situation is invaluable. Not only will you see the offense and the offender more clearly, but he'll give you a new perspective on yourself as well. Many times, I find that when I get the Father's perspective on the offense I see that it was my own brokenness, my own previous opinion of myself that allowed for the offense. As a matter of fact, let's look at my pitfall and see what the Father showed me when I asked him for his perspective. Here's what he said:

> Robin, your heart still suffers from feeling rejected and unwanted. Release your friend. The communication between you was normal and healthy. Sheila misunderstood Amy's plans and communicated an idea to you that wasn't really going to work. This is just a misunderstanding that was innocent and not meant to be hurtful. I know the retracting of the invitation hit

the rejection that still rings in your ears and tells you who you are. But listen to me. I'm telling you that you are mine—wanted, received, invited, and loved. Receive my love.

Isn't that good? I love hearing my Dad talk to me. He loves me so much!!

Why don't you try it? Ask Daddy God to give you his perspective on the situation you've been working through. Ask the Holy Spirit to speak to you.

_____

_____

_____

_____

_____

_____

_____

_____

_____

_____

_____

FOLLOW THE PATH

We have done some great work together! We have recognized a painful memory and the wound that it agreed with. We've also identified the trap the enemy meant to ensare us with of slavery or orphanhood. We have gained victory over that painful memory and release from the bondage of unforgiveness. Thank you Jesus!!

Now I'm going to show you how to use the same tools, with the help of the Holy Spirit, to continue following the map of your memories as far back as he will allow. Why do you need to do this? Well, if there is more hurt in your history, then there is likely more unforgiveness, and if there is unforgiveness then there is imprisonment and torment, and if those two have been allowed then we know access to your life has been given to the enemy. If he has access what will he do? Well, simply put, whatever he can to steal, kill and destroy you. At every turn he'll try to reset his traps for orphanhood and slavery in your life.

Where do we start? With questions of course! Let's stay with the wound that we dealt with in the last situation if the Holy Spirit will let us. Ask him if there is another painful memory that he wants to bring up that collides with the same wound.

I'll be guinea pig again. My wound was rejection. I asked the Holy Spirit for another memory and he gave me one immediately.

It was Friday night in the fall, which means football, the social gathering of the week. Two of my girlfriends and I had put a plan together for the evening. The plan began with them coming to pick me up for the game and then ended with a post-game hangout together with some other friends. They were running fifteen minutes late, but I figured they were probably getting all primped for the night. No big deal; we'd still make it to half-time. Thirty minutes past kickoff and still no friends. The night went on, the game was over, and still no friends. I finally got a hold of them at one girl's house (this was before cell phones or you know I'd have been calling them earlier!). I asked what had happened, why didn't they come get me? She responded that she had just forgotten about me. I hung up the phone and cried. I felt so unimportant, unwelcome, unwanted.

Just like in the previous exercises I walked out the steps to pinpoint my compulsive responses, recognize my wound, identify the lies, traps, vows, and unforgiveness I had taken into my heart as a result of this hurt.

Now it's your turn. From here on you can use the tools I've given you to identify the hurtful situations, recognize the wound that ignites the compulsive response, identify the traps and pinpoint the vows you've made. The next tools are forgiveness, repentance, and blessing. Each step is outlined below just like we did them together earlier. I pray for the Holy Spirit to guide you on your journey ahead to seek out the pitfalls, and I bless you to learn to trust your guide even more with every step you take. The following pages allow you to use this exercise to process any situation the Holy Spirit might bring to your mind.

The Hurtful Situation (Healing Exercise #1)

Ask your guide, "Holy Spirit, take me to a memory of a hurtful circumstance, conversation, or encounter that you want to deal with where my internal need to protect myself took over and I reacted to something in an almost involuntary way."

Write down the event, conversation or interaction in detail.

_____

_____

_____

_____

_____

_____

The Compulsive Response

Can you remember having a desire to defend yourself in that situation? Did you go through an automatic cycle of thoughts or feelings? Were there compulsive plans to retaliate, payback, or prove something to that person? Or, like me, did you have any compulsive reactions to the situation? Write down your compulsive response. It may have been physical, emotional, or mental.

_____

_____

_____

Now ask the Holy Spirit to help you understand what you were defending and/or preserving with those compulsive actions.

_____

_____

_____

_____

_____

_____

The Wound

Examine the situation again. Write down what happened in brief again. Ask the Holy Spirit to bring light to your memory and to show you what your wound is.

_____

_____

_____

_____

_____

_____

Ask the Holy Spirit to bring his light and connect any dots necessary to see what was really happening.

_____

_____

Ask the Holy Spirit to speak to your heart about this wound. Ask him to show you where it could have started or another memory that it is connected to. Write out what he shows you.

_____

_____

_____

_____

_____

_____

_____

_____

_____

The Trap

Ask the Holy Spirit to come and bring his light into your heart to show you if you've let this wound become a confession. Write your conclusion and any "I am" statements below.

_____

_____

_____

_____

Ask the Holy Spirit to reveal what trap the enemy was trying to ensnare you in with this wound. Was it orphanhood or slavery or some mixture of the two?

_____

_____

_____

Ask the Holy Spirit to reveal all of the lies the enemy trapped you into believing about the Father and his character. Write them below.

_____

_____

_____

_____

Now, let's make some confessions that will begin to work against the enemy's plans for you. Ask the Holy Spirit to speak his truth into the wound you've suffered from. What does he say about you? Write it below.

_____

_____

_____

_____

Now take what the Holy Spirit said to you about yourself and write new "I am" statements of truth.

_____

_____

The Father is so good and wants to rescue us from the traps we've fallen into. Ask the Holy Spirit to speak to you about who you are, the truth. You can begin by writing the "I am" statement he gave you earlier, but ask him to tell you more.

_____

_____

_____

_____

Ask the Holy Spirit to tell you who the Father is to you.

_____

_____

_____

_____

As we did earlier, this is a good time for you to repent of the agreements you made with the enemy about yourself and the Father and renounce them. I have a prayer written below, but ask the Holy Spirit to guide you through your prayer and give you new insight and words to fully release yourself from the contract you made with the enemy about your identity. This is a wonderful time to practice your prayer language as well and let the Holy Spirit minister to the deepest places that are past your natural mind.

Prayer of Repentance

Father, I recognize that I have not seen myself the way that you do. I have let the situations of my life tell me who I am. I've believed these messages so much that I've even enabled this belief to become my truth and my reality by admitting that I am (write your false "I am" statement):

_____

_____

_____

_____

I repent of confessing that about myself. I know that it was sin because it was in opposition of what you say is true about me. It was also sin because in that place in my heart I haven't received your love. I renounce my agreement with the enemy that I am (write the trap you have fallen into—an orphan, a slave, both?)

_____

_____

And I repent of believing that you are (write the lies about the Father):

_____

_____

So, now, I speak out the truth that you say that I am (write your "I am" statement of truth):

_____

_____

Because I am free of those lies I can now say that you, Father, really are (write who the Father told you he was):

_____

_____

I need the Holy Spirit to help me remember who I am. I choose to speak this truth to myself over and over even if I don't feel like it is true. It really is true! *I am your favorite son! I am your favorite daughter!*

Vow of Protection

Ask the Holy Spirit to help you see the vow you made in your heart when you received hurt. Don't assume you didn't make one; it could be subtle like mine. Write what he shows you below.

_____

_____

_____

_____

_____

Ask the Holy Spirit to show you the thought process that led you to make that vow.

_____

_____

_____

_____

_____

Prayer of Renunciation

Now renounce the vow you made and break the power it has had over your life. Let's pray, "Father, I break the vow I made (write out the vow):

_____

_____

_____

_____

Now, I apply Jesus' blood to the vow and I renounce the vow completely in the name of Jesus. I refuse to agree any longer with the thoughts that caused me to make that vow. I don't need to vow anything any longer because Jesus has come to show me his love—your love for me. You receive me completely as I am, and I don't need to believe anything other than what you say about me.

The Offense

Write down the hurtful point of the situation. Ask the Holy Spirit to reveal any subtleties that you may not see in the situation that will help the offense become clear. What do you hear?

_____

_____

_____

_____

The Offender

Who is the person behind the hurt? Ask the Holy Spirit to reveal if there is more than one. Write their names below:

_____

_____

_____

Prayer of Forgiveness

Father, I am your son/daughter and I want to love others as you have loved me. I choose to forgive (name the offenders):

_____

_____

I forgive them for the offense of (name the offense):

_____

_____

They don't owe me anymore for the hurt that they caused me. I do not hold them responsible for the wound (name the wound):

_____

_____

I suffered this wounding, whether intentional or unintentional, from them, but now I release them to be blessed by your hand. I ask that you stop the reaping of the unforgiveness I've partnered with and

remove me from the bondage and torment I've placed myself under by participating in unforgiveness. Thank you for the gift of Jesus and his blood that covers me. I receive that covering and place it between me and the offense.

The Father's Perspective

Ask Daddy God to give you his perspective on the situation you've been working through. Write what he tells you below:

_____

_____

_____

_____

_____

_____

_____

_____

_____

_____

The Hurtful Situation (Healing Exercise #2)

Ask your guide, "Holy Spirit, take me to a memory of a hurtful circumstance, conversation, or encounter that you want to deal with where my internal need to protect myself took over and I reacted to something in an almost involuntary way."

Write down the event, conversation or interaction in detail.

_____

_____

_____

_____

_____

The Compulsive Response

Can you remember having a desire to defend yourself in that situation? Did you go through an automatic cycle of thoughts or feelings? Were there compulsive plans to retaliate, payback, or prove something to that person? Or, like me, did you have any compulsive reactions to the situation? Write down your compulsive response. It may have been physical, emotional, or mental.

_____

_____

_____

Now ask the Holy Spirit to help you understand what you were defending and/or preserving with those compulsive actions.

_____

_____

_____

_____

_____

_____

The Wound

Examine the situation again. Write down what happened in brief again. Ask the Holy Spirit to bring light to your memory and to show you what your wound is.

_____

_____

_____

_____

_____

_____

Ask the Holy Spirit to bring his light and connect any dots necessary to see what was really happening.

_____

_____

Ask the Holy Spirit to speak to your heart about this wound. Ask him to show you where it could have started or another memory that it is connected to. Write out what he shows you.

_____

_____

_____

_____

_____

_____

_____

_____

_____

_____

The Trap

Ask the Holy Spirit to come and bring his light into your heart to show you if you've let this wound become a confession. Write your conclusion and any "I am" statements below.

_____

_____

_____

_____

Ask the Holy Spirit to reveal what trap the enemy was trying to ensnare you in with this wound. Was it orphanhood or slavery or some mixture of the two?

_____

_____

_____

Ask the Holy Spirit to reveal all of the lies the enemy trapped you into believing about the Father and his character. Write them below.

_____

_____

_____

_____

Now, let's make some confessions that will begin to work against the enemy's plans for you. Ask the Holy Spirit to speak his truth into the wound you've suffered from. What does he say about you? Write it below.

_____

_____

_____

_____

Now take what the Holy Spirit said to you about yourself and write new "I am" statements of truth.

_____

_____

The Father is so good and wants to rescue us from the traps we've fallen into. Ask the Holy Spirit to speak to you about who you are, the truth. You can begin by writing the "I am" statement he gave you earlier, but ask him to tell you more.

_____

_____

_____

_____

Ask the Holy Spirit to tell you who the Father is to you.

_____

_____

_____

_____

As we did earlier, this is a good time for you to repent of the agreements you made with the enemy about yourself and the Father and renounce them. I have a prayer written below, but ask the Holy Spirit to guide you through your prayer and give you new insight and words to fully release yourself from the contract you made with the enemy about your identity. This is a wonderful time to practice your prayer language as well and let the Holy Spirit minister to the deepest places that are past your natural mind.

Prayer of Repentance

Father, I recognize that I have not seen myself the way that you do. I have let the situations of my life tell me who I am. I've believed these messages so much that I've even enabled this belief to become my truth and my reality by admitting that I am (write your false "I am" statement):

_____

_____

_____

_____

I repent of confessing that about myself. I know that it was sin because it was in opposition of what you say is true about me. It was also sin because in that place in my heart I haven't received your love. I renounce my agreement with the enemy that I am (write the trap you have fallen into—an orphan, a slave, both?)

_____

_____

And I repent of believing that you are (write the lies about the Father):

_____

_____

So, now, I speak out the truth that you say that I am (write your "I am" statement of truth):

_____

_____

Because I am free of those lies I can now say that you, Father, really are (write who the Father told you he was):

_____

_____

I need the Holy Spirit to help me remember who I am. I choose to speak this truth to myself over and over even if I don't feel like it is true. It really is true! *I am your favorite son! I am your favorite daughter!*

Vow of Protection

Ask the Holy Spirit to help you see the vow you made in your heart when you received hurt. Don't assume you didn't make one; it could be subtle like mine. Write what he shows you below.

_____

_____

_____

_____

_____

Ask the Holy Spirit to show you the thought process that led you to make that vow.

_____

_____

_____

_____

_____

Prayer of Renunciation

Now renounce the vow you made and break the power it has had over your life. Let's pray, "Father, I break the vow I made (write out the vow):

_____

_____

_____

_____

Now, I apply Jesus' blood to the vow and I renounce the vow completely in the name of Jesus. I refuse to agree any longer with the thoughts that caused me to make that vow. I don't need to vow anything any longer because Jesus has come to show me his love—your love for me. You receive me completely as I am, and I don't need to believe anything other than what you say about me.

The Offense

Write down the hurtful point of the situation. Ask the Holy Spirit to reveal any subtleties that you may not see in the situation that will help the offense become clear. What do you hear?

_____

_____

_____

_____

The Offender

Who is the person behind the hurt? Ask the Holy Spirit to reveal if there is more than one. Write their names below:

_____

_____

_____

Prayer of Forgiveness

Father, I am your son/daughter and I want to love others as you have loved me. I choose to forgive (name the offenders):

_____

_____

I forgive them for the offense of (name the offense):

_____

_____

They don't owe me anymore for the hurt that they caused me. I do not hold them responsible for the wound (name the wound):

_____

_____

I suffered this wounding, whether intentional or unintentional, from them, but now I release them to be blessed by your hand. I ask that you stop the reaping of the unforgiveness I've partnered with and

remove me from the bondage and torment I've placed myself under by participating in unforgiveness. Thank you for the gift of Jesus and his blood that covers me. I receive that covering and place it between me and the offense.

The Father's Perspective

Ask Daddy God to give you his perspective on the situation you've been working through. Write what he tells you below:

_____

_____

_____

_____

_____

_____

_____

_____

_____

_____

_____

_____

The Hurtful Situation (Healing Exercise #3)

Ask your guide, "Holy Spirit, take me to a memory of a hurtful circumstance, conversation, or encounter that you want to deal with where my internal need to protect myself took over and I reacted to something in an almost involuntary way."

Write down the event, conversation or interaction in detail.

_____

_____

_____

_____

_____

_____

The Compulsive Response

Can you remember having a desire to defend yourself in that situation? Did you go through an automatic cycle of thoughts or feelings? Were there compulsive plans to retaliate, payback, or prove something to that person? Or, like me, did you have any compulsive reactions to the situation? Write down your compulsive response. It may have been physical, emotional, or mental.

_____

_____

_____

Now ask the Holy Spirit to help you understand what you were defending and/or preserving with those compulsive actions.

_____

_____

_____

_____

_____

_____

The Wound

Examine the situation again. Write down what happened in brief again. Ask the Holy Spirit to bring light to your memory and to show you what your wound is.

_____

_____

_____

_____

_____

_____

Ask the Holy Spirit to bring his light and connect any dots necessary to see what was really happening.

Ask the Holy Spirit to speak to your heart about this wound. Ask him to show you where it could have started or another memory that it is connected to. Write out what he shows you.

The Trap

Ask the Holy Spirit to come and bring his light into your heart to show you if you've let this wound become a confession. Write your conclusion and any "I am" statements below.

_____

_____

_____

_____

Ask the Holy Spirit to reveal what trap the enemy was trying to ensnare you in with this wound. Was it orphanhood or slavery or some mixture of the two?

_____

_____

_____

Ask the Holy Spirit to reveal all of the lies the enemy trapped you into believing about the Father and his character. Write them below.

_____

_____

_____

_____

Now, let's make some confessions that will begin to work against the enemy's plans for you. Ask the Holy Spirit to speak his truth into the wound you've suffered from. What does he say about you? Write it below.

_____

_____

_____

_____

Now take what the Holy Spirit said to you about yourself and write new "I am" statements of truth.

_____

_____

The Father is so good and wants to rescue us from the traps we've fallen into. Ask the Holy Spirit to speak to you about who you are, the truth. You can begin by writing the "I am" statement he gave you earlier, but ask him to tell you more.

_____

_____

_____

_____

Ask the Holy Spirit to tell you who the Father is to you.

_____

_____

_____

_____

As we did earlier, this is a good time for you to repent of the agreements you made with the enemy about yourself and the Father and renounce them. I have a prayer written below, but ask the Holy Spirit to guide you through your prayer and give you new insight and words to fully release yourself from the contract you made with the enemy about your identity. This is a wonderful time to practice your prayer language as well and let the Holy Spirit minister to the deepest places that are past your natural mind.

Prayer of Repentance

Father, I recognize that I have not seen myself the way that you do. I have let the situations of my life tell me who I am. I've believed these messages so much that I've even enabled this belief to become my truth and my reality by admitting that I am (write your false "I am" statement):

_____

_____

_____

_____

I repent of confessing that about myself. I know that it was sin because it was in opposition of what you say is true about me. It was also sin because in that place in my heart I haven't received your love. I renounce my agreement with the enemy that I am (write the trap you have fallen into—an orphan, a slave, both?)

_____

_____

And I repent of believing that you are (write the lies about the Father):

_____

_____

So, now, I speak out the truth that you say that I am (write your "I am" statement of truth):

_____

_____

Because I am free of those lies I can now say that you, Father, really are (write who the Father told you he was):

_____

_____

I need the Holy Spirit to help me remember who I am. I choose to speak this truth to myself over and over even if I don't feel like it is true. It really is true! *I am your favorite son! I am your favorite daughter!*

Vow of Protection

Ask the Holy Spirit to help you see the vow you made in your heart when you received hurt. Don't assume you didn't make one; it could be subtle like mine. Write what he shows you below.

_____

_____

_____

_____

_____

Ask the Holy Spirit to show you the thought process that led you to make that vow.

_____

_____

_____

_____

_____

Prayer of Renunciation

Now renounce the vow you made and break the power it has had over your life. Let's pray, "Father, I break the vow I made (write out the vow):

_____

_____

_____

_____

Now, I apply Jesus' blood to the vow and I renounce the vow completely in the name of Jesus. I refuse to agree any longer with the thoughts that caused me to make that vow. I don't need to vow anything any longer because Jesus has come to show me his love—your love for me. You receive me completely as I am, and I don't need to believe anything other than what you say about me.

The Offense

Write down the hurtful point of the situation. Ask the Holy Spirit to reveal any subtleties that you may not see in the situation that will help the offense become clear. What do you hear?

_____

_____

_____

_____

The Offender

Who is the person behind the hurt? Ask the Holy Spirit to reveal if there is more than one. Write their names below:

_____

_____

_____

Prayer of Forgiveness

Father, I am your son/daughter and I want to love others as you have loved me. I choose to forgive (name the offenders):

_____

_____

I forgive them for the offense of (name the offense):

_____

_____

They don't owe me anymore for the hurt that they caused me. I do not hold them responsible for the wound (name the wound):

_____

_____

I suffered this wounding, whether intentional or unintentional, from them, but now I release them to be blessed by your hand. I ask that you stop the reaping of the unforgiveness I've partnered with and

remove me from the bondage and torment I've placed myself under by participating in unforgiveness. Thank you for the gift of Jesus and his blood that covers me. I receive that covering and place it between me and the offense.

The Father's Perspective

Ask Daddy God to give you his perspective on the situation you've been working through. Write what he tells you below:

_____

_____

_____

_____

_____

_____

_____

_____

_____

_____

WALKING INTO SONSHIP

DIVINE GIFTS

As we heal, it will become more and more apparent that we were made to be enjoyed by the Father and to enjoy the life he gave us to live. For some this may not be a huge revelation, but for others who have lived under the heavy weight of orphanhood and slavery this will be very freeing. Some have suffered from the lack of confidence that orphanhood brings, never knowing who they are or never feeling like they were endorsed and approved by their Father. Some have labored under the burden of slavery, too busy trying to please the master and earn their way into his favor to understand that he delights in them already and wants them to savor this life!

Here's a new motto for us to embrace: Sonship is about being yourself! Orphanhood is about searching, slavery is about earning, sonship is about being. It will help you to be yourself if you know yourself really well. When we're living our lives out of the heart of the orphan and the slave, we are constantly searching for an identity; therefore, we don't really know ourselves. As a orphan or a slave, we learn who we are by achievement and approval or by morphing into whatever is necessary to be accepted. But we are sons! Let's walk on in our journey and learn more about ourselves.

Remember earlier when we talked about the Father giving gifts to each of us and the fact that we are gifts to other people as well? We discovered in Psalm 139 that he wove us together. Let's look at that scripture a little closer.

> My frame was not hidden from you when I was made in the secret place. When I was woven together in the depths of the earth, your eyes saw my unformed body. All the days ordained for me were written in your book before one of them came to be. (Psalm 139:15-16)

We established earlier that the depths of the earth was the spirit realm. And if he formed us in the secret place, what part of us was he forming there? Verse 13 says, "For you created my inmost being; you knit me together in my mother's womb." We can see that in our mother's womb he knit together our flesh and bone, our natural being. But what was he making in the secret place, in "the depths of the earth?" Could it have been our spirit man?

What is our spirit man? It is the part of us that is unseen. It is our soul, our heart, our gifts, our capacities, and our abilities. He created these in the depths of the earth, in the secret place. He did not create them in the natural. So where did he get those parts of us that he wove together? Did he draw them from the atmosphere? No, he drew them from himself. Amazing. Think about what the psalmist is describing: all of our unseen parts were formed out of the Father himself in the spirit realm, where he exists completely. This means that all of your gifts and capacities, all of the things that make you you, are from the Father. And they are not just a gifts he gives, but they are part of who he is! Isn't that amazing? So your gifting in math, sports, crafts, cooking, business, marketing, building, speaking, singing, teaching, and on and on, is from within himself: "For from him and through him and to him are all things. To him be the glory forever! Amen" (Romans 11:36).

So what does this mean for us? Well, besides the grand gesture of his kindness that is giving to us such wonderful gifts, it means that there is not a gift in us that is not important, since he is all important. And there is not a gift in us that is not meant to bless others, since he loves and blesses us all. And every gift in us is meant to bring eternal value to his kingdom, since it is his kingdom.

In the healthiest and most whole places in our lives we graciously operate in our gifts. In those places we are able both to receive praise for excellent execution of our gifts and give honor to the Father who gave us these gifts. However, there are many times when we don't act so graciously. What do we do instead? We do one of two things. We either devalue our gifts by not receiving or recognizing them, or we swing the opposite direction and find our personal worth and value in them and therefore elevate them to a place of worship. Why do we devalue them when they are so beautifully a part of who the Father is in us? Or conversely, why do we promote our gifts above where they should be promoted in our lives? Well, you can probably guess what I'm going to say? It is a part of our struggle to move out of orphanhood and slavery. If you found yourself getting slightly depressed right now because you recognized that you either reduce or promote your gifts don't worry! We just acquired new tools for our tool kit in the last chapters and you, my friend, are on your journey to a life lived from the position of a son instead of an orphan or slave. We're moving into a healed place in the kingdom and we're receiving the Father's love in those places that were waxed. So let's look at how a healthy soul can live completely inside of who God made him or her to be as sons and function in the gifts he gave to him or her.

GIFTS ARE TOOLS FOR LOVING

Just to give it some language, I believe that when we elevate a gift above its proper place we treat it like a trophy. Instead of being used to love others as it was intended, the gift is set up high where others can see it and admire that we have it. The opposite is true when we devalue a gift. When we diminish a gift we treat it like a toy. It becomes something that we can play with, but it is unimportant. In both of these cases we miss the eternal nature of the gift. We are also less likely to take the impact of the gift on others seriously; therefore, we operate in it out of our own strength and direction instead of out of partnership with the Father. However, when we recognize that the gift is not only a treat for us but also a blessing to others, we see it as a tool in our hands. One that is satisfying to wield and beneficial to the ones who receive it.

I believe God gave us gifts for two reasons. The first and foremost is that he loves us. Any good Father gives his children gifts because he loves them and it is his good pleasure to give them. There is a quote in the movie *Chariots of Fire* that is one of my favorites. In the scene, Eric Liddell, born in China to Scottish missionaries, has been accepted to represent Britain in the 1924 Olympic games in Paris. His sister Jennie objects to his plans to compete in the games, but he sees running as a way to glorify God before returning to China to continue his work as a missionary. When Eric accidentally misses a church prayer meeting because of his training, his sister Jennie chastises him and charges him with no longer caring about God. Eric informs her that though he will return to the Chinese mission field, he feels divinely energized when he runs and that not to run would be dishonoring to God. It is at this point that he says, "I believe God made me for a purpose, but he also made me fast. And when I run I feel his pleasure." Eric was expressing the heart of a son: "My Dad is pleased with me already, and when I run I feel his pleasure because I'm expressing what he made me to do and enjoy." Isn't that great? I love that. I want to live like that more and more in my own life.

The second reason the Father gave us gifts is so that we can use them to love people and bless others. He outfitted you perfectly. Did you know that? He gave you the perfect set of gifts that not only work together, but that work with other parts of you as well. The Father so perfectly wove you together that your gifts work with your personality, your abilities, and your physical and emotional capacities. You were meant not only to enjoy the work of your hands, but to bless and love others with your work as well.

This idea is seen beautifully in the movie *Chocolat,* in which a chocolatier wanders with her daughter across France. In the winter of 1959, the two settle in a tranquil French village where the mother opens a chocolaterie. The store stirs up both admiration and anxiety in the minds of the villagers, as it opens during the forty days of Lent. The mayor, oppressed by religion, presses his religion on everyone in town. But the chocolatier won't receive that pressure; instead, she sets about enjoying the work of her hands and loving the people of the village with her creations. If you have eyes to see you'll recognize a theme throughout the movie: Do what you love, and love others with your abilities. By the end of the movie we see that because she simply focused her gifts on people, the lives of people around her changed. People's lives change when any person uses his or her gifts to love, whether he or she is a believer or not. Imagine, though, what happens when sons and daughters who've submitted those gifts to the partnership and direction of the Father begin loving people with their gifts. The beauty of the kingdom comes forth and it makes an eternal impact.

DISCOVERING OUR GIFTS

Recognizing why we've been given gifts is our first move on our pathway to destiny. The next step is discovering and uncovering the gifts that are within us. I think most people would be surprised at the exhaustive list of gifts and capacities that the Father has woven into them. When we can begin to grasp and articulate the gifts and capacities within us, we can better steward our time, plan our schedules, and love our people.

Many times we burn out because we are doing things we were not created to do. I know that sounds simplistic, but it's true. And this is not to say that we should not do anything that isn't fun or that we should not do anything that is hard work. In fact, it is more fun to work hard at something we love to do and are willing to make sacrifices for. We will all face hardships and trials, but wouldn't we rather encounter trials while doing the things we love to do and that we have grace for instead of while doing things we despise and have no capacity for? Let's dig in and see what God has woven into us!

Gifts

Gifts are talents or skills that you can perform, like drawing, carving, decorating, managing, or planning. Likewise, abilities are skills you can perform, as well. However, abilities are things you can do but that you wouldn't maybe consider a "gift," like cleaning. Cleaning may not be glamorous, but it is definitely a gift!

Write down all the gifts and abilities you can think of that you operate in presently. It doesn't matter whether or not you feel that you excel at them currently; write them down anyway.

_____

_____

_____

_____

_____

_____

_____

_____

Capacities

Knowing your capacities is having an awareness of your limits or how much of one thing or another you can handle. Knowing your limits is important when it comes to stewarding your gifts and your time. You may be great at hosting large crowds, while someone else has a great capacity for solitude. Maybe you love to travel and have a capacity to learn languages easily.

Write down the capacities that you recognize in yourself. This is your potential to deal with or handle a certain thing or things.

_____

_____

_____

_____

Spiritual Gifts

There is another kind of gift that I haven't mentioned yet, and that is a spiritual gift. Let's look at some scripture just to kick us off:

> To one there is given through the Spirit the message of wisdom, to another the message of knowledge by means of the same Spirit, to another faith by the same Spirit, to another gifts of healing by that one Spirit, to another miraculous powers, to another prophecy, to another distinguishing between spirits, to another speaking in different kinds of tongues, and to still another the interpretation of tongues. All these are the work of one and the same Spirit, and he gives them to each one, just as he determines. (1 Corinthians 12:8-11)

It is clear from this passage that these are gifts that are supplied to us by the Father at his choosing, and they all come by the Spirit.

Ask the Holy Spirit to reveal to you the spiritual gifts that he's already given you and write them down in the lines below.

_____

_____

_____

_____

We are invited to ask for other spiritual gifts that we don't currently operate in. As Paul encourages two chapters later, "eagerly desire spiritual gifts" (1 Corinthians 14:1). Have you asked for spiritual gifts? Have you ever felt that it is greedy for you to ask for more gifts when you know the Father has already given you some? Well, if spiritual gifts are all meant for building one another up and encouraging one another, then how is it greedy to ask for more?

Let's approach the Father as sons and desire for more. Write down any spiritual gifts that you would like to operate in. Then ask the Father to give them to you. We are encouraged to ask for what we want.

_____

_____

_____

_____

Isn't it fun to see those things on paper? We've made room in this book for you to do that exercise three more times. You can do it once a quarter, if you will, for the next year. I think you'll be amazed to see how just being aware of what gifts are in you makes you more apt to use them.

THE FATHER'S GIFTS

Both our natural gifts and our spiritual gifts are the Father's gifts. They came from him, they flow through us, and when we love others with them they glorify him. Let's submit all of the gifts we have named to the Father and ask him to bless us, the gifts, and those who will be loved through them.

"Father, you are so good to me. Thank you for filling me with such beautiful treasures. I receive all of these gifts and I submit them to you, your care, and your will for my life."

This is space for you to practice your listening prayer by asking the Father questions about your gifts. Here are some to get you started. First, write down one of your gifts that you would like to hear from the Father about:

_____

_____

Let's ask the question, "Father, how do you feel about this gift you gave to me?" Now write what you hear from the Father.

_____

_____

"Is this a good season to pursue using this gift?

_____

_____

_____

"Where do you see me using it and is there someone I could partner with?

_____

_____

_____

_____

"What group of people have you already wired me to love with this gift?

_____

_____

_____

"What can I do to be better equipped in this gift?"

_____

_____

_____

I HAVE DESTINY IN MY FATHER

Our destiny is our future in God, who states very clearly that he has made plans for us. We read in Jeremiah 29:11, "'For I know the plans I have for you,' declares the Lord, 'plans to prosper you and not to harm you, plans to give you hope and a future.'" And here in Psalm 33:11 we read, "But the plans of the Lord stand firm forever, the purposes of his heart through all generations."

I believe that we were "fearfully and wonderfully made," as Psalm 139:14 tells us, and I believe that all of the gifts and capacities that the Father wove into us were meant to work in concert to fulfill our destiny in God.

When it comes to fulfilling our destiny, many people ask how they know if they are doing it right. If the kingdom is a family, then fulfilling our destiny must be about the same thing. And in the simplest terms, family is about "with-ness." The question isn't necessarily about fulfilling our destiny, it's about whether or not we are we pursuing our destiny and fulfilling it *with* the Father. Friendship, partnership, family—these are the kingdom. Notice, words like successful, mega- and profitable aren't in that list. Now that doesn't mean that with the Father our efforts won't succeed, grow or bring financial increase. On the contrary, they just might do those very things. But fulfilling our destiny isn't about that. It's about being *with* the Father, being beside him, being able to say, "Hey Dad, watch this." My two boys are incredibly creative, smart and playful, and sharing life with them means that there is always something to watch. Isn't that what our heart wants? To be seen by God? If we always try to be perfect and get it right (oh, the suffering slave heart) or if we get our identity from our gifts (oh, the suffering orphan heart) then we won't want to be seen until we are perfect, or at least presentable. And what does that say about our hearts and our relationship to God? It says that we believe he won't really receive us unless we're performing well or unless we *are* something. A son just wants to be seen, to be watched, to be *with*.

Have you struggled with trusting the Father with your gifts? Do you believe he has the best plans for you, or have you wondered if you got the short end of the stick at times? Turn the page and journal your confessions to him. Ask the Holy Spirit to bring light and revelation to you about your heart.

_____

_____

_____

_____

_____

_____

_____

_____

_____

_____

If we haven't trusted the Father with our gifts or trusted that he has good plans for us, then we probably haven't been in the "with" mindset when it comes to accomplishing things with our gifts. Ask the Father to reveal any places in your life in which you've been reluctant to release your process to him, places where you wanted to accomplish the goal and show him the finished product instead of letting him be with you. Write what he tells you in the lines that follow:

_____

_____

_____

_____

_____

_____

_____

_____

_____

If you've struggled in either one of these areas, repent of having mistrust for the Father. Mistrust certainly stems from the roots we've been talking about, the questions seeded into hearts in the garden. I've written a guided prayer to help you, but ask the Holy Spirit to bring revelation to what is really happening in your heart and give you words to pray.

"Father, I repent from not trusting you completely with my gifts and my process of accomplishing things. I also repent for not believing you had wonderful plans for my future. I know that is a part of the enemy's desire and plan to draw my heart away from you. I want to trust you. Please heal the parts of my heart that can't receive your goodness right now so that I can trust you completely."

THE ENEMY OF MY DESTINY

If you want to understand your destiny with more clarity, look at where the enemy has pointed his arrows. They will be in direct opposition to your destiny. Earlier in the book we determined that the enemy hates us not because we impact his kingdom of darkness or cause him trouble. He hates us simply because we are the Father's beloved sons. This is the same reason he is out to steal our destiny from us. As 1 Peter 5:8 reads, "Your enemy the devil prowls around like a roaring lion looking for someone to devour. So be self-controlled and alert." We need to be aware of what he's out to destroy. Can he actually steal our destiny? I don't believe so. Can he steal our salvation? Absolutely not. But can he lie to us about who we are so that we never have the confidence in our identity in Christ to take hold of our destiny and see it come to pass? Yes.

Let me tell you a little story to help this make sense. I am not an intellectual; I've struggled my whole life with feeling stupid. I have memories of trying to do flash cards in math. My older sister was doing hers with my mom, and my dad had mine laid out in choo-choo train fashion on the floor. My sister was banging through her cards like lightening. I could hear my mom in the next room: "Good! great!" The announcement of my mother's approval as my sister gave the correct answers made me nervous. I hadn't finished one card! My dad was losing his patience with me and I can imagine why: "There are 3 apples on the cart. You add 2 more. Now how many apples are on the cart?" Why was it so hard for me? I still don't know why I struggled so much. But what I do know is that the "I am" statement that was reinforced that day was "I am stupid." That was the lie the enemy desired to seed into my heart that day, and the next ten years of public school (where my learning style was not employed) would prove to compound that lie. That seed was watered and fertilized in my heart year after terrible year.

Now, why did the enemy need to tell me I'm stupid? He could have told me so many other things. But he had a clue of what my destiny was in the Father. He could read the signs of what he saw in me, that I would be a writer, a teacher, and a leader. I can imagine what the enemy was thinking; "What better way to keep her down than to convince her that she could never do those things because she is stupid?" Here's a news flash: I am still battling that lie. Almost every other day—definitely weekly—something happens in my world that wants to agree with that lie. And so I continue to do warfare against it. Speaking the truth of who I am and the destiny that I believe is before me. Not because I *feel* smart but because I know my God-given gifts are threatening to the enemy. Why else would he try so hard to keep them down? Attaining our destiny requires a trust in the character of our Father, a belief in his goodness, and a vision for the future that only sons can possess. We can only live fully into our destiny when we live as sons.

Did my story trigger any memories for you? Do you have your own story of being discouraged in a certain pursuit? Take time to write it down below. Ask the Holy Spirit to illuminate any details you might not have seen before that could be important to understanding the enemy's plans against your destiny.

Ask the Holy Spirit to show you what that discouragement and negative message was meant to destroy. What point of my destiny was the enemy trying to prevent from coming to full bloom?

_____

_____

_____

_____

_____

_____

_____

_____

_____

Let's thank the Father for his plans for our destiny and his provision at every turn: "Father you know the beginning from the end and I'm thankful that you have a plan for my future and that you made me with a destiny in mind. I'm thankful that my destiny is in you and will be fulfilled with you! I will not fear because I know the enemy can't steal my destiny. I trust you because you are good to me."

OUR DREAMS, OUR DESTINY

I grew up believing that the destiny or "call" of God on my life would be something outside of myself. I believed it was something that I should do, but most likely that it was not something I wanted to do. I think this thinking was based on the teaching I often heard about doing work for God, making sacrifices for his work, and dying to self. This must be where ideas like "sowing your wild oats" comes from—If you're not going to do anything fun with God you'd better do it now without him! The teaching I received bred a feeling in me that my desires and dreams were carnal and fleshly and definitely not from God. That's why I thought his plans for me would always require sacrifice and that in dying to myself and my flesh, I would have to let my dreams die as well.

Here's some good news: I was wrong! The good news that I never heard growing up was that the dreams I had for myself were the Father's dreams, and he had given them to me. When Jesus saved me he redeemed every part of me, my dreams included. And when the Father was weaving me in the spirit realm he not only wove in gifts and capacities, but he also wove in his own dream threads as well. Some people have a hard time with that picture because they see how some people use their gifts and dreams and ambitions for selfish, or even wicked, purposes. This is true. A person whose gifts and dreams are left unredeemed will surely focus some, if not all, of these on themselves or on wickedness. But we are talking about believers, his sons, who are redeemed by the blood of Jesus. And that means all parts of us, dreams included!

So, armed with that awesome knowledge, let's see what our dreams look like on paper. Don't let anything get in your way; let your mind be free in the presence of the Holy Spirit and trust that your dreams are his. Let's take some time and write out some dream statements. Turn the page and begin.

"These are my dreams for my family:

_____

_____

_____

_____

"These are my dreams for my career:

_____

_____

_____

_____

"These are my dreams in helping others:

_____

_____

_____

_____

"These are my dreams for how I will use my gifts:

_____

_____

_____

_____

"This is something I have dreamed of doing since childhood:

_____

_____

_____

_____

"This is a new dream God has dropped into my heart recently."

_____

_____

_____

_____

This is a wonderful start. What you will see as you trust your dreams to the Father is that he will take whatever parts that are still based in your flesh and change them to agree with his Spirit. He's just that good!

MOVING TOWARD MY DREAMS

You can still move toward pursuing your destiny even though you are waiting for the Lord's direction, unless of course he has told you specifically not to move on something. Isn't it true that if your car is out of gas it's easier to get it to the gas station if you can start it rolling? An object in motion is easier to turn and redirect than one that is sitting still.

So get moving! Try something! Even if your attempt fails, at least you will have stepped out and learned something about yourself, your gift, and the Lord in the process. Give yourself opportunities for what I like to call "godly experiments." These are attempts at something we love to do in full view of the Father, with or without divine direction. In godly experiments, we enjoy the fact that God wove our gifts into us and we decide to give them a whirl and see what he does. If you experiment in full view of the Father, then you can hear him tell you to do things like *change this, do this, don't do that, that's not a good choice, this is a better approach* and it won't break your spirit because you know he loves you. It's true, if we suffer from slavery we will have a harder time experimenting because we can only enjoy our own successes and we can't stand to get correction or redirection. We must remember that we please the Lord when we fail as well as when we succeed! We please him just because we are his, not because of what we do or how well we do it.

I love it when my boys draw and paint. Xander excels in this department. I watch him color and give detail, line, and shape to a thing, and it is satisfying to my heart. But it is satisfying not because he is excelling, but because it satisfies his heart to be creative. I love what he loves because I love him.

Write some ways you can experiment and take steps toward your dreams. Take one of your dreams from the previous section and write one thing you could do this month toward accomplishing that dream.

_____

_____

_____

_____

_____

Think about your childhood dreams. Are you doing anything relating to them now? If not, what could you do that would point you in that direction?

_____

_____

_____

_____

_____

Is there dissonance between your plans for career and your plans for family? If so, ask the Holy Spirit what you could change this month that would put you on a new trajectory for the future. Turn the page and write it down.

_____

_____

_____

_____

_____

_____

DISCOVERING OUR GIFTS

I've made room for you to revisit this exercise again in a few months. I encourage you to take these questions and use them again and again as time goes by to allow the Father to reveal more of the beautiful treasure that you are.

Gifts

Write down all the gifts and abilities you can think of that you operate in presently. It doesn't matter whether or not you feel that you excel at them currently; write them down anyway.

_____

_____

_____

_____

_____

_____

_____

_____

_____

Capacities

Write down the capacities that you recognize in yourself. This is your potential to deal with or handle a certain thing or things.

_____

_____

_____

_____

_____

_____

_____

Spiritual Gifts

Ask the Holy Spirit to reveal to you the spiritual gifts that he's already given you.

_____

_____

_____

Write down any spiritual gifts that you would like to operate in. Then ask the Father to give them to you if it's his will.

_____

_____

_____

"Father, you are so good to me. Thank you for filling me with such beautiful treasures. I receive all of these gifts and I submit them to you, your care, and your will for my life."

This is space for you to practice your listening prayer by asking the Father questions about these gifts. Here are some to get you started.

"How do you feel about my gifting in . . .? (Write the gift.)

_____

_____

_____

_____

"Is this a good season to pursue using this gift?

_____

_____

_____

_____

"Where do you see me using it and is there someone I could partner with?

_____

_____

_____

_____

"What group of people have you already wired me to love with this gift?"

_____

_____

_____

CONTINUE TO WALK
IN HIS FAVOR

DESTINY

The Father loves us as his favorite sons. Now it is time to live like we believe that we are.

We can live in victory over the lies of the enemy even if we haven't uncovered them all yet. It is true. We just have to claim the truth of who we are, the truth of our favor in God. Say this with me: "I am my Father's favorite son/daughter." In the beginning a statement like this can sound forced to our ears. I know it did to mine. But Matthew 12:34 says that "out of the overflow of the heart the mouth speaks." Matthew 15:18 says, "but the things that come out of the mouth come from the heart." So first we have to help our hearts believe the truth by confessing the truth with our mouths. Say it with me again: "I am my Father's favorite son/daughter."

The first time that phrase left my lips I did all kinds of arguing about how I couldn't be his favorite. I quoted scripture about how he didn't show favoritism, and then I argued with myself some more. So how did it stick, you might ask? Well, I'm an experiential learner, and the Lord knows this about me. One night when I was tucking my boys into bed I said, "Xander, you are my favorite boy in the world." And I heard Zane ask quietly, "Am I your favorite, too?" To which I replied without even thinking, "Of course you are! There's no one else like you in the world. You are my favorite, too." I stopped and stared for a minute because I was getting it for the first time, as well. My Dad made me unique from everyone else on the earth, and there is no one else like me. I am his favorite! He can say I am his favorite just like I could honestly say that Zane and Xander were both my favorites! I love them the same, with as much love as I can give them. They can't win more love from me or more favor. They can win more privileges and more trust, but they cannot win more love or more favor. They have those because they are my boys; they belong in my heart!

All of that is true for you with your heavenly Father. Can you hear that for yourself? You can't win a better place with the Father; you can't win more love or less love! You are unique and irreplaceable to the Father. You are his favorite you!

I pray that your heart is swelling even now with excitement at the love the Father has for you. You take up acreage in his heart that belongs to no one else. You are unique and he made you the way you are for a reason. The plans of the enemy will not prevail against you! I proclaim it for you!

I encourage you to continue on this journey, this hike along the pathway to sonship. All of your effort is worth the pain of revisiting hurtful memories. Your effort is leading you to become who you really are: a son. Don't give up. Sometimes it will feel as if you're repeating a turn you've taken before or as if you've seen a pitfall more than once. Don't give up. And don't get discouraged if you find you are dealing with a wound that you thought you had already conquered or a trap you thought you were already freed from. Take time to notice that you're looking at these places from a new perspective. You've moved beyond that original site to a higher place, and now you have understanding and wisdom you didn't have the first time.

Take the tools that I've given you, the messages of truth I've proclaimed to you, and claim them for yourself. Keep writing your notes, keep asking more questions of the Holy Spirit, keep searching the depths of the Father's love for you. And most of all, as Paul encourages us in Philippians 3:14, keep pressing on "toward the goal to win the prize for which God has called [you] heavenward in Christ Jesus"—to our destiny as sons and daughters.

www.robinpasley.com

CPSIA information can be obtained at www.ICGtesting.com
Printed in the USA
BVOW070551030112

279647BV00001B/6/P